AIRPORT
SPOTTING GUIDE

Far East and Australasia

MATT FALCUS

First Edition 2011

Cover design by John Wright

ISBN 978-0-9567187-1-6

© 2011 Matthew Falcus

British Library Cataloguing-in-Publication Data

A catalogue record for this book is available from the British Library.

Published by Destinworld Publishing Ltd.

www.destinworld.com

Front cover photograph © Peter Spence

Contents

Airports in Indonesia

Airports in Japan

Airports in Malaysia & Singapore

Airports in New Zealand

Airports in Philippines

Airports in South Korea

Airports in Thailand

Introduction

The Far East can be one of the most exhilarating areas to visit for the aviation enthusiast. Air transport in this part of the world plays an important part in everyday lives, with domestic networks in the likes of China and Japan still incredibly popular and affordable, and covering vast networks. China in particular has many airlines operating from hundreds of airports, with more opening every year, and its biggest airlines are accepting new aircraft at a pace not seen elsewhere in the world.

Also included in this title are the main airports in Australia and New Zealand – two countries incredibly popular with European and North American holidaymakers. Aircraft spotting and photography is quite a popular pastime in these countries and many airports provide areas to watch movements. There are also a number of museums and restoration projects related to aviation. What's more, in Australia the sunny weather and warm climate can make the hobby incredibly enjoyable and produce some excellent photographs.

Japan is another country that provides for aircraft enthusiasts, with observation decks at almost all airports, no matter how small. For this reason, spotters come back again and again to Japan to pursue their hobby.

China on the other hand is less welcoming to the hobby in most, but not all, places. Very few official viewing areas are provided at airports and security personnel will often question and move on spotters. Photography of aircraft is also officially not allowed, although with care some snaps can be taken. However, at the country's bigger airports such as Beijing Capital (the world's second busiest airport), spotting is tolerated and catered for.

Where China disappoints in official spotting locations, it excels in its aviation museums which allow you to wander and photograph as much as you want. Datangshan in Beijing is a fantastic collection of civil airliners and military aircraft from various eras, and of types that are rarely found anywhere else.

This book intends to provide the spotter visiting Australasian and Far Eastern airports with an all-inclusive collection of guides to the biggest, busiest and most interesting airports. The details are taken from the author's own visits and trusted sources. Whilst every attempt has been made to ensure details are correct, the nature of airports and laws on spotting mean that details are likely to change over time, and you must use discretion where necessary and always check with authorities that you are permitted to spot and photograph aircraft. I hope you will find useful recommendations in this book. Happy spotting!

Matt Falcus

This page has been intentionally left blank.

Commercial Airports by Country

This list gives details of the principal commercial airports in each country of the Far East and Australasia where you can expect to find regular airline and cargo flights.

AUSTRALIA

Adelaide (ADL/YPAD)
Alice Springs (ASP/YBAS)
Ayers Rock/Yulara (AYQ/YAYE)
Brisbane International (BNE/YBBN)
Broome International (BME/YBRM)
Canberra International (CBR/YSCB)
Cairns International (CNS/YBCS)
Carnarvon (CVQ/YCAR)
Coffs Harbour (CFS/YFCS)
Darwin International (DRW/YPDN)
Geraldton (GET/YGEL)
Gold Coast/Coolangatta (OOK/YBCG)
Gove (GOV/YPGV)
Hamilton Island (HTI/YBHM)
Hobart International (HBA/YMHB)
Kalgoorlie-Boulder (KGI/YPKG)
Karratha (KTA/YPKA)
Kununurra (KNX/YPKU)
Launceston (LST/YMLT)
Learmouth (LEA/YPLM)
Lord Howe Island (LDH/YLHI)
Mackay (MKY/YBMK)
Melbourne Avalon (AVV/YMAV)
Melbourne Essendon (MEB/YMEN)
Melbourne International (MEL/YMML)
Melbourne Moorabbin (MBW/YMMB)
Mount Isa (ISA/YBMA)

Newcastle Williamtown (NTL/YWLM)
Norfolk Island (NLK/YSNF)
Perth (PER/YPPH)
Port Hedland (PHE/YPPD)
Portland (PTJ/YPOD)
Rockhampton (ROK/YWIS)
Sunshine Coast (MCY/YBMC)
Sydney Bankstown (BWU/YSBK)
Sydney Kingsford Smith International (SYD/YSSY)
Toowoomba (TWB/YTWB)
Townsville (TSV/YBTL)
Wagga Wagga (WGA/YSWG)

CHINA

Baotou (BAV/ZBOW)
Beihai (BHY/ZGBH)
Beijing Capital International (PEK/ZBAA)
Beijing Nanyuan (NAY/ZBNY)
Changchun Longjia International (CGQ/ZYCC)
Changde (CGD/ZGCD)
Chengdu Shuangliu International (CTU/ZUUU)
Changsha Huanghua International (CSX/ZGHA)
Chifeng (CIF/ZBCF)
Chongqing Jiangbei International (CKG/ZUCK)
Dalian Zhoushuizi International (DLC/ZYTL)
Datong (DAT/ZBDT)
Fuzhou Changle International (FOC/ZSFZ)
Ganzhou (KOW/ZSGZ)
Guangyuan (GYS/ZUGU)
Guangzhou Baiyun International (CAN/ZGGG)
Guilin Liangjiang International (KWL/ZGKL)
Guiyang Longdongbao International (KWE/ZUGY)
Haikou Meilan International (HAK/ZJHK)
Hangzhou Xiaoshan International (HGH/ZSHC)
Harbin Taiping International (HRB/ZYHB)
Hefei Luogang International (HFE/ZSOF)
Hohhot Baita International (HET/ZBHH)

Hong Kong Chep Lap Kok (HKG/VHHH)
Huangshan Tunxi International (TXN/ZSTX)
Huangyan Luqiao (HYN/ZSLQ)
Ji'an (JGS/ZSJA)
Jinan Yaoqiang International (TNA/ZSJN)
Jingdezhen (JDZ/ZSJD)
Jiujiang Lushan (JIU/ZSJJ)
Kunming Wujiaba International (KMG/ZPPP)
Lanzhou West (LHW/ZLLL)
Lianyuangang Baitabu (LYG/ZSLG)
Lijang (LJG/ZPLJ)
Linyi (LYI/ZSLY)
Liuzhou (LZH/ZGZH)
Luoyang (LYA/ZHLY)
Luzhou (LZO/ZULZ)
Macau International (MFM/VMMC)
Mianyang Nanjiao (MIG/ZUMY)
Mudanjiang (MDG/ZYMD)
Nanjing Lukou International (NKG/ZSNJ)
Nanchang International (KHN/ZSCN)
Nanning Wuxu International (NNG/ZGNN)
Nanyang (NNY/ZHNY)
Ningbo Lishe International (NGB/ZSNB)
Ordos Dongsheng (DSN/ZBDS)
Qingdao Liuting International (TAO/ZSQD)
Quanzhou Jinjiang (JJN/ZSQZ)
Quzhou (JUZ/ZSJU)
Qianjiang Zhoubai (under construction)
Sanya Phoenix International (SYX/ZGSY)
Shanghai Hongqiao International (SHA/ZSSS)
Shanghai Pudong International (PVG/ZSPD)
Shantou Waisha (SWA/ZGOW)
Shenyang Taoxian International (SHE/ZYTX)
Shenzhen Bao'an International (SZX/ZGSZ)
Shijiazhuang Daguocun International (SJW/ZBSJ)
Taiyuan Wusu (TYN/ZBYN)

Tianjin Binhai International (TSN/ZBTJ)
Ürümqi Diwopu International (URC/ZWWW)
Wanzhou Wuqiao (WXN/ZULP)
Weihai (WEH/ZSWH)
Wenzhou International (WNZ/ZSYW)
Wuhai (WUA)
Wuhan Tianhe International (WUH/ZHHH)
Xi'an Xianyang International (XIY/ZLXY)
Xiamen Gaoqi International (XMN/ZSAM)
Xiangfan (XFN/ZHXF)
Xining Caojiabu (XNN/ZLXN)
Yanji Chaoyangchuan (YNJ/ZYYJ)
Yantai Laishan International (YNT/ZSYT)
Yibin (YBP/ZUYB)
Yinchuan Hedong (INC/ZLIC)
Yiwu (YIW/ZSYW)
Yulin (UYN/ZLYL)
Yuncheng (YCU/ZBYC)
Zhangjiajie Dayong (DYG)
Zhanjiang (ZHA/ZGZJ)
Zhengzhou Xinzheng International (CGO/ZHCC)
Zhuhai International (ZUH/ZGSD)
Zuxhou Guanyin (XUZ/ZSXZ)

INDONESIA

Ambon Pattimura (AMQ/WAPP)
Balikpapan Syamsudin Noor (BPN/WALL)
Banda Aceh Blang Bitang (BTJ/WITT)
Bandung Husein Sastranegara International (BDO/WICC)
Banjarmasin Syamsudin Noor (BDJ/WAOO)
Batam Hang Nadim (BTH/WIDD)
Denpasar Bali International (DPS/WADD)
Jakarta Halim International (HLM/WIIH)
Jakarta Soekarno-Hatta International (CGK/WIII)
Jayapura Sentani (DJJ/WAJJ)
Kendari Wolter Monginsidi (KDI/WAWW)
Kupang Eltari (KOE/WATT)

Manado Sam Ratulangi (MDC/WAMM)
Maumere Wai Oti (MOF/WATC)
Medan Polonia International (MES/WIMM)
Padang Minankabau International (PDG/WIPT)
Palangkara Panarung (PKY/WAOP)
Pekanbaru Simpang Tiga (PKU/WIBB)
Semarang Achmad Yani (SRG/WARS)
Solo City Adi Sumarmo Wiryokusumo (SOC/WARQ)
Sorong Jefman (SOQ/WASS)
Surabaya Juanda International (SUB/WARR)
Tembagapura Timika (TIM/WABP)
Ujung Pandang Sultan Hasanuddin International (UPG/WAAA)
Yogyakarta Adisutjipto (JOG/WARJ)

JAPAN

Akita (AXT/RJSK)
Aomori (AOJ/RJSA)
Asahikawa (AKJ/RJEC)
Fukuoka (FUK/RJFF)
Fukushima (FKS/RJSF)
Hakodate (HKD/RJCH)
Kagoshima (KOJ/RJFK)
Kita Kyushu (KKJ/RJFR)
Kobe (UKB/RJBE)
Komatsu (KMQ/RJNK)
Kumamoto (KMJ/RJFT)
Matsuyama (MYJ/RJOM)
Memambetsu (MMB/RJCM)
Miyazaki (KMI/RJFM)
Nagasaki (NGS/RJFU)
Nagoya Chubu Centrair International (NGO/RJGG)
Nagoya Komaki (NKM/RJNA)
Niigata (KIJ/RJSN)
Oita (OIT/RJFO)
Okayama (OKJ/RJOB)
Osaka Itami International (ITM/RJOO)
Osaka Kansai International (KIX/RJBB)

Sendai (SDJ/RJSS)
Sapporo New Chitose International (CTS/RJCC)
Shizuoka (FSZ/RJNS)
Takamatsu (TAK/RJOT)
Tokyo Haneda (HND/RJTT)
Tokyo Narita (NRT/RJAA)
Toyama (TOY/RJNT)

MALAYSIA
Bintulu (BTU/WBGB)
Johor Bahru Senai International (JHB/WMKJ)
Kota Kinabalu International (BKI/WBKK)
Kuala Lumpur International Airport (KUL/WMKK)
Kuala Lumpur Sultan Abdul Aziz Shah (SZB/WMSA)
Kuching International (KCH/WBGG)
Labuan (LBU/WBKL)
Miri (MYY/WBGR)
Penang International (PEN/WMKP)
Sandakan (SDK/WBKS)
Sibu (SBW/WBGS)
Tawau (TWU/WBKM)

NEW ZEALAND
Auckland International (AKL/NZAA)
Blenheim Woodbournet (BHE/NZWB)
Chatham Islands Tuuta (CHT/NZCI)
Christchurch International (CHC/NZCH)
Dunedin International (DUD/NZDN)
Gisborne (GIS/NZGS)
Hamilton International (HLZ/NZHN)
Nelson (NSN/NZNS)
New Plymouth (NPL/NZNP)
Palmerston North International (PMR/NZPM)
Queenstown (ZQN/NZQN)
Rotorua (ROT/NZRO)
Taupo (TUO/NZAP)
Tauranga (TRG/NZTG)

Wanganui (WAG/NZWU)

Wellington International (WLG/NZWN)

PHILIPPINES

Busuanga Francisco B. Reyes (USU/RPVV)

Catarman National (CRM/RPVF)

Francisco Bangoy (Davao) International (DVO/RPMD)

General Santos (Tambler) International (GES/RPMR)

Ilo-Ilo International (ILO/RPVI)

Kalibo International (KLO/RPVK)

Legazpi (LGP/RPLP)

Luzon Island Diosdado Macapagal International (CRK/RPLC)

Mactan-Cebu International (CEB/RPVM)

Manila Ninoy Aquino International (MNL/RPLL)

Puerto Princesa International (PPS/RPVP)

Zamboanga International (ZAM/RPMZ)

SINGAPORE

Paya Lebar Air Base (QPG/WSAP)

Singapore Changi International (SIN/WSSS)

Singapore Seletar (XSP/WSSL)

SOUTH KOREA

Busan Gimhae International (PUS/RKPK)

Cheongju International (CJJ/RKTU)

Daegu International (TAE/RKTN)

Jeju International (CJU/RKPC)

Muan International (MWX/RKJB)

Seoul Gimpo International (GMP/RKSS)

Seoul Incheon International (ICN/RKSI)

TAIWAN

Kaohsiung International (KHH/RCKH)

Taichung (RMQ/RCMQ)

Taipei Songshan (TSA/RCSS)

Taipei Taoyuan International (TPE/RCTP)

This page has been intentionally left blank.

Airports in Australia

1. Adelaide Airport
2. Brisbane Airport
3. Darwin Airport
4. Melbourne International Airport
5. Perth Airport
6. Sydney Kingsford Smith International Airport

This page has been intentionally left blank.

Adelaide Airport, Australia

ADL | YPAD

Tel: +61 8 8308 9211
Web: www.adelaideairport.com.au
Passengers: 7,000,000+ (2010)

Overview

Adelaide is the fifth busiest airport in Australia. Its new international terminal was built as recently as 2005 after the previous building was found to be severely restricted in space. The new building earned the airport an award as one of the best international airports in the world. The old terminal still serves domestic flights.

Although traffic is not as busy as at other Australian airports, you will still see a good mix of domestic, international and cargo airlines here. The airport acts as a hub for Qantas and Tiger Airways Australia. There is also a busy general aviation and FBO ramp to the north of the terminals.

Spotting Locations

1. Tapley's Car Park

This official viewing spot is located close to the threshold of runway 05. It is a small parking area off the A15 (Tapleys Hill Rd) road, opposite the golf course. You are fairly close to aircraft using the runway and taxiing by, but the airport fence can restrict photographs somewhat. It is free to park here.

2. Airport Bike Track

The Airport Bike Track runs around much of the eastern and southern perimeter of the airport, so you can happily walk or cycle to a good spot and watch the action. There are some good photography spots, too, but beware of the heat and lack of shade on hot days. The path runs from Lew St to James Montrose Rd with various access points along the way.

3. James Schofield Drive

This access road runs from the airport entrance to the various GA, cargo and maintenance areas to the north of the terminals. Although you shouldn't loiter, you can get some useful views for logging and photographing aircraft parked out of the way.

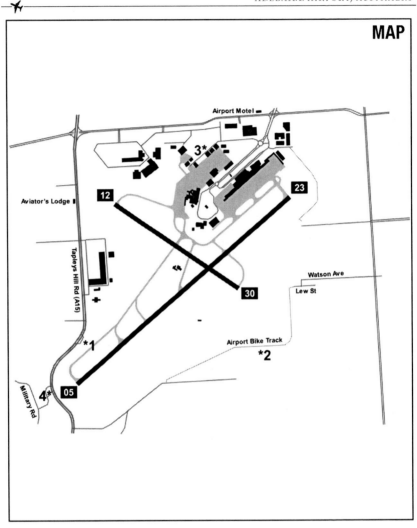

MAP

Airport Motel
Aviator's Lodge
Tapleys Hill Rd (A15)
Military Rd
Watson Ave
Lew St
Airport Bike Track

3*
12
23
*1
30
*2
4* 05

Frequencies

Tower	120.5
Ground	121.7
Clearance Delivery	126.1
Arrival/Departure	118.2
Arrival/Departure	124.2
Arrival/Departure	128.6
ATIS	116.4
ATIS	134.5

Runways

05/23	10,171ft / 3,100m
12/30	5,420ft / 1,652m

4. Airport Lookout

Close to the first location is another lookout spot near the end of runway 05. It is situated in a car park off the road linking Tapleys Hill Rd and Military Rd, between the golf course and the Patawalonga River. It has a slightly elevated view over the airfield, and is excellent for landing shots on 05.

Airlines

Airlines
Air New Zealand
Alliance Airlines
Cathay Pacific
Cobham
Jetstar Airways
Malaysia Airlines
Pacific Blue
Qantas
Qantas (QantasLink)
Regional Express Airlines
Sharp Airlines
Singapore Airlines
Singapore Airlines Cargo
Tiger Airways Australia
Toll Priority
Virgin Blue

Hotels

Comfort Inn Aviator's Lodge

728 Tapleys Hill Road, Adelaide, SA 5024 | +61 8 8356 8388 | www.aviatorslodge.com.au

A pleasant little hotel that is affordable and modern. It is situated just across the road from the perimeter fence, opposite the domestic terminal and cross runway. Rooms don't have views, but you don't have to venture far outside to see movements.

Adelaide Airport Motel

406 Sir Donald Bradman Dr, Brooklyn Park, SA 5032 | +61 8 8234 4000
www.adelaideairportmotel.com.au

Located very close to the new International Terminal just outside the airport entrance. Again, no views of movements but it's not far to go to get them. Affordably priced and has free shuttle to the terminals.

Nearby Attractions

Adelaide Parafield Airport

Adelaide's former main airport is Parafield, situated north of the city centre and around 12 miles from the current main airport. It has four short runways, and today operates principally as a general aviation airfield. Views can be had from the various roads running around the perimeter. It is also home to an aviation museum:

Classic Jets Fighter Museum

Hangar 52, Anderson Drive, Parafield Airport, SA | +61 8 8258 2277 | www.classicjets.com

A collection of RAAF and RAN jet aircraft from the 1950s to 1980s all on display for close inspection. These include a P38H Lockheed Lightning, Gloster Meteor, Dassault Mirage III, De Havilland Sea Venom and Tiger Moth amongst others. Open daily from 10am-4pm (3pm on Monday and Tuesday). Adults $9, Children 5-15 $4.50, Seniors $7.50, Under 5's free

Brisbane Airport, Australia

BNE | YBBN

Tel: +61 7 3406 3000
Web: bne.com.au
Passengers: 19,059,718 (2009)

Overview

Brisbane Airport is the largest and busiest in Queensland, on Australia's eastern coast. It is the third busiest in Australia and served by the main operators in the country, along with plenty of overseas airlines. Qantas send their Airbus A330 and Boeing 767 fleets here for maintenance. Alliance Airlines, QantasLink and VirginBlue also perform maintenance here. The original airport site is now the cargo area, whilst maintenance is done on the opposite side of the main runway to the two terminals.

Spotting Locations

1. International Terminal

An observation deck is provided in the International Terminal on the top level. It is a good spot for watching movements, particularly if using runway 01. Photography is possible with a good lens.

2. Acacia Street

A small parking area and raised concrete slab makes this a nice spot for watching aircraft on the main and secondary runways, as well as taxiing to and from the terminals. You won't miss much here, although the fence makes it a little difficult to take unobstructed photographs. to reach the spot, turn left at the roundabout next to the control tower onto Dryanda Rd, then turn right onto Acacia St and follow to the end.

3. Fire Station

On the opposite side of the airfield, this is a good spot to see what's in the maintenance hangars and also to photograph aircraft on the main runway with the Brisbane skyline as a backdrop. To get there, head towards the city from the terminals and take a left onto Lomandra Dr. At the end turn left onto Myrtletown Rd. Turn left onto Pandanus Ave, and then left again onto Baeckea St. Park in the car park.

MAP

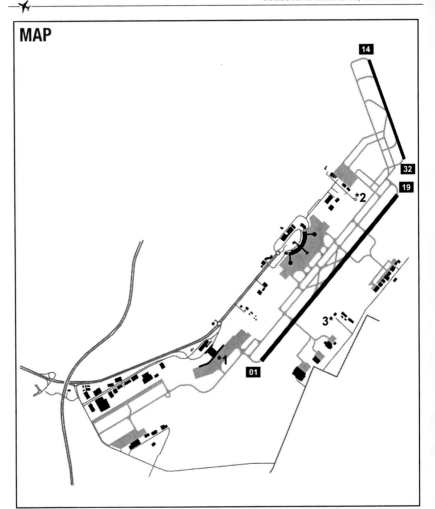

Frequencies

Tower	120.5
Ground	121.7
Clearance Delivery	118.6
Radar	125.7
Departures (NW)	128.3
Approach (NW)	124.7
Approach (Gold Coast)	123.5
Approach (SE)	125.6
Radar	125.7
ATIS	113.2
ATIS	125.5

Runways

01/19 11,680ft / 3,560m
14/32 5,577ft / 1,700m

Airlines

Air New Zealand	Norfolk Air
Air Niugini	Our Airline
Air Pacific	Pacific Air Express
Air Vanuatu	Pacific Blue
Aircalin	Polynesian Blue
Australian Air Express	Qantas
Brindabella Airlines	Qantas (Alliance Airlines)
Cathay Pacific	Qantas (Jetconnect)
China Airlines	Qantas (QantasLink)
China Eastern Airlines	Royal Brunei
China Southern Airlines	Singapore Airlines
DHL (Pel-Air)	Skytrans Airlines
Emirates	Solomon Airlines
Etihad Airways	Strategic Airlines
EVA Air	Thai Airways International
Garuda Indonesia	Tiger Airways Australia
HeavyLift Cargo Airlines	Toll Aviation (Jetcraft Aviation)
Jetstar Airways	Toll Priority
Korean Air	V Australia
Malaysia Airlines	Virgin Blue

Hotels

Novotel Brisbane Airport

The Circuit, Brisbane Airport QLD 4009 | (07) 3175 3100 | www.accorhotels.com

The closest hotel to the terminals at Brisbane is the Novotel, which is affordable and comfortable. You'll be lucky to find any room with a view of aircraft movements, however.

Nearby Attractions

Southern Cross

This historic aircraft was the first to fly across the pacific (with Charles Kingsford Smith at the helm). It is now preserved in a special hangar just outside the International Terminal at Brisbane Airport.

Queensland Air Museum

Caloundra Aerodrome, 7 Pathfinder Drive, Caloundra QLD | (07) 5492 5930 | www.qam.com.au

Situated almost 60 miles north of Brisbane is Caloundra Aerodrome, which is used by GA traffic. It is also the home of this small museum with a number of preserved civil and military aircraft. Open daily (except Christmas) 10am-4pm. Adults $10, Concession $8, Child $6.

This page has been intentionally left blank.

Darwin, Australia

DRW | YPDN

Tel: +61 8 8920 1811
Web: www.darwinairport.com.au
Passengers: 1,813,000 (2007)

Overview

Darwin is a joint civil-military airport in Australia's Northern Territory. It is the country's 10th busiest airport and handles many domestic flights and some international flights to nearby South-East Asia (although Garuda recently suspended flights here). As well as the civil operations, the RAAF operates a variety of military aircraft, from F-16 fighter jets to large Hercules and KC-135 tankers through the airport.

To the north west of the terminal is a large GA area which is very busy with light aircraft, business jets and some historic aircraft. Darwin also has a cargo terminal which regularly handles aircraft up to Boeing 747 size.

Spotting Locations

1. Terminal

The departures area of the terminal has good views over the ramp and main runway. Although through glass, photography is fine for anything close up. Head for the smoking room for the best views.

2. Aviation Museum

From the car park of the Australian Aviation Heritage Centre, off Stuart Highway, you have good views of aircraft shortly before landing on runway 29.

3. Bagot Road

This road runs down the western perimeter of the airport and has a variety of shops and eateries with car parks. You can find a good spot near Baggins from which to watch aircraft arriving on runway 11.

MAP

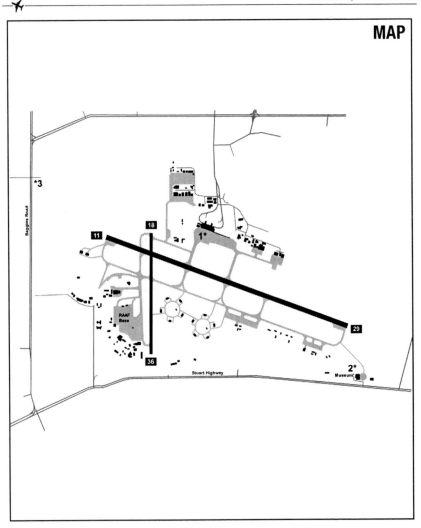

Frequencies

Tower	133.1
Ground	119.55
Ground	121.8
Clearance Delivery	126.8
Departure	123.0
Approach	125.2
Approach	134.1
ATIS	112.6

Runways

11/29	11,004ft / 3,354m
18/36	5,000ft / 1,524m

Airlines

Airnorth
Indonesia AirAsia
Jetstar Airways
Qantas
Qantas (QantasLink)
Skywest Airlines
Tiger Airways Australia
Vincent Aviation
Virgin Blue

Hotels

Darwin Airport Inn

Cnr Henry Wrigley Drive & Sir Norman Brearley Drive, Marrara NT | +61 8 8920 7900 | www.darwinairportinn.com.au

A popular, well-equipped resort hotel as well as a night-stop for those using the airport. Some rooms offer distant views either south to the terminal and main runway, or west towards the GA parking area.

Nearby Attractions

Australian Aviation Heritage Centre

Stuart Highway, Winnellie NT 0821 | +61 8 8947 2145 | www.darwinsairwar.com.au

Sited on the southern boundary of Darwin Airport, this is one of the best aviation museums in Australia. It is home to a complete B-52 bomber, plus a number of other military and civil types. It also holds many aircraft engines and various photographic, weapons and wartime artefact displays. Open every day, 9am-5pm with tours at 10am. Adults $12, Seniors $9, Under-12 $7, Family $30, Student $7.50.

This page has been intentionally left blank.

Melbourne Airport, Australia

MEL | YMML

Tel: +61 3 9297 1600
Web: www.melbourneairport.com.au
Passengers: 26,287,000 (2009)

Overview

Melbourne is Australia's second-busiest airport and a major hub for Qantas. Jetstar Airways, Regional Express and Tiger Airways Australia also make up a large proportion of the airport's movements. There are numerous places around the airport to watch aircraft movements, and the weather usually makes for some good photographs.

There are four passenger terminals at the airport, plus a cargo terminal. The airport has won numerous awards over the years and is pleasing to pass through. Despite its size and popularity, the city's second airport - Avalon (see Nearby Attractions) - has been expanding in recent years and is now set to take on international flights also.

Spotting Locations

1. Northern Viewing Area

Where Oaklands Rd joins route C743 there is a small parking area for spotters. At this spot you are just underneath the final approach path to runway 16. It is a bit distant to see much of the rest of the airport.

2. Operations Rd Viewing Area

Another designated viewing area is on Operations Rd along the airport's western perimeter. You are alongside runway 16/34 here, and have views across to the terminals. It is a bit distant, and you'll need a ladder to get any useful shots.

3. Southern Perimeter

Alongside Operations Rd on the southern perimeter is a good spot for photographing arrivals on runway 34. You will also see aircraft taxiing for takeoff. Plenty of spotters congregate at this location.

MAP

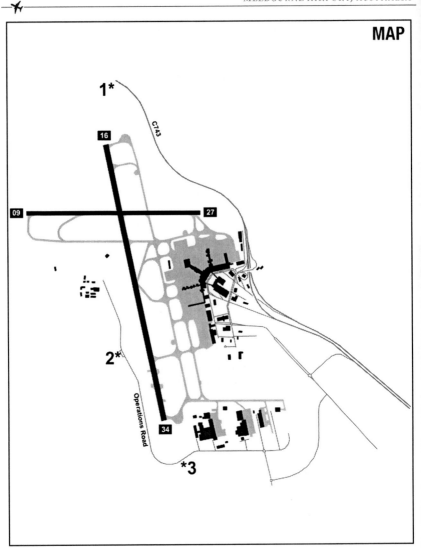

Frequencies

Ground	121.7
Tower	120.5
Departures	118.9 (264-092)
Departures	129.4 (093-263)
Approach	132.0
ATIS	114.1
ATIS	132.7
Clearance Delivery	127.2

Runways

09/27	7,500ft / 2,286m
16/34	11,998ft / 3,657m

Airlines

Air China	Norfolk Air (Our Airline)
Air Mauritius	Pacific Blue
Air New Zealand	Philippine Airline
Air Pacific	Qantas
Air Vanuatu	Qantas (Jetconnect)
AirAsia X	Qantas (QantasLink)
Atlas Air	Qatar Airways
Australian air Express	Regional Express
Cathay Pacific	Royal Brunei
Cathay Pacific Cargo	Singapore Airlines
China Eastern Airlines	Singapore Airlines Cargo
China Southern Airlines	Skywest Airlines
Emirates	Thai Airways International
Etihad Airways	Toll Priority
Garuda Indonesia	Toll Priority (Jetcraft Aviation)
Jetstar Airways	United Airlines
Korean Air	V Australia
Malaysia Airlines	Vietnam Airlines
MASkargo	Virgin Blue

Hotels

Hilton Airport Hotel

Arrival Drive, Melbourne Airport, Melbourne 3045 | +61 3 8336 2000 | www.hilton.com

You can walk directly into this hotel from the terminals via covered walkway. Rooms can be a bit pricey, but some have excellent views over the airport. Ask for those in the ranges 800-825 and 900-925. You can also get views from the ends of the corridors.

Nearby Attractions

Melbourne Avalon Airport

Situated around 30 miles south-west of Melbourne city centre, Avalon is the city's second-busiest airport. It has a single runway and flights operated by Jetstar Airways, Sharp Airlines and Tiger Airways Australia. Qantas also send their aircraft here for heavy maintenance. The Australian International Airshow is held at Avalon every two years. Aircraft parked at the terminal and approaching the runway can easily be seen from the car park and Airport Dr. Alternatively, to see aircraft at the Qantas hangars, head east on Beach Rd, then turn right onto Pousties Rd.

Melbourne Essendon Airport

This was formerly Melbourne's first international airport, opened in the 1920s. It is located 4 miles from the current Melbourne International Airport. Today it is still an important gateway for business and light aircraft, and has some local flights operated by Sharp Airlines.

Melbourne Moorabbin Airport

One of Australia's busiest GA and business airports. It is located in southern Melbourne, around 13 miles from the centre of the city. It also serves flights by King Island Airlines. Many of the parked aircraft can be seen from First Ave and Northern Ave. The airport is also home to the Australian National Aviation Museum.

The Australian National Aviation Museum

1 Second Ave, Moorabbin Airport, Victoria 3194 | +61 3 9580 7752 | www.aarg.com.au

Australian National Aviation Museum, or Moorabbin Museum, is a great museum located close to the airport terminal. It houses a nice selection of preserved wartime aircraft, jets, and classic airliners. These include a DC-2, DC-3, Vickers Viscount, Bristol Freighter and de Havilland Heron. The museum is open Wednesday to Friday 12-4pm, and Saturday, Sunday & public holidays 10am-5pm. Adults $7.50, Children/Concessions/Students $3.50 (under 5's free).

Perth Airport, Australia

PER | YPPH

Tel: +61 8 9478 8888
Web: www.perthairport.net.au
Passengers: 10,463,971 (2009)

Overview

Perth is the busiest airport in Western Australia and a major hub for domestic travel as well as links throughout Asia and to Africa and the Middle East. A nice mix of airlines serve the airport, though naturally Australian carriers dominate. Also, due to the amount of mining operations in this part of Australia, Perth Airport handles large numbers of charter flights supporting these activities.

The airport has three terminals - two domestic and an international terminal, which are separated on either side of the two runways. The International Terminal caters for spotters from its viewing deck, however the domestic side of the airport is home to a variety of ramps and hangars which feature business and GA aircraft, and often aircraft in storage or maintenance. The cargo terminal is also on the domestic side.

As Perth has experienced passenger growth, it is anticipated the airport will expand further and eventually see a combined domestic and international terminal developed on the eastern side. In the meantime the current facilities will be upgraded.

Spotting Locations

1. International Terminal Viewing Deck

Atop the International Terminal, on the eastern side of the airport, is the official viewing area. The views are perfect for any aircraft using that terminal, and you can see all movements on the runways. However, you are some distance from aircraft using the domestic terminal.

2. The Mound

On the domestic side of the airport, if you arrive via the Great Eastern Highway, exit onto Fauntleroy Ave, and then turn 2nd left onto Bungana Ave. Along here you'll find the mount with views over the parking areas for business jets and FBO's, and some distant views of the runways and domestic terminal.

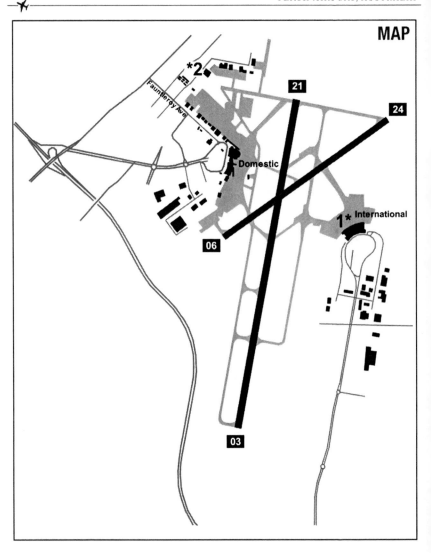

MAP

Frequencies

Tower	120.5
Ground	121.7
Radar	135.25
Clearance Delivery	118.55
Clearance Delivery	132.95
Departure	118.7
Approach	123.6
ATIS	113.7
ATIS	123.8

Runways

03/21	11,299ft / 3,444m
06/24	7,096ft / 2,163m

Airlines

Air Mauritius
Air New Zealand
AirAsia
AirAsia X
Airnorth
Alliance Airlines
Australian Air Express
Batavia Air
Cathay Pacific
Cobham
Emirates
Garuda Indonesia
Indonesia AirAsia
Jetstar Airways
Malaysia Airlines
Maroomba Airlines

Network Aviation
Pacific Blue
Qantas
QantasLink (Cobham)
Royal Brunei
Singapore Airlines
Skippers Aviation
Skywest Airlines
South African Airways
Star Aviation
Strategic Airlines
Thai Airways International
Tiger Airways
Tiger Airways Australia
Toll Priority
Virgin Blue

Hotels

Marracoonda Airport Motel

375 Great Eastern Highway, Redcliffe, WA 6104 | +61 8 9479 1521

A small motel very conveniently located for Perth Airport. Situated around a mile from the Domestic Terminal. Rooms do not have views of any movements, but the hotel has all the amenities you'd need and is affordable.

Nearby Attractions

RAAF Pearce

This is a large air base around 20 miles north of Perth, at the town of Bullsbrook. It is principally used as a training base for the Royal Australian Air Force and Republic of Singapore Air Force, however fighter jets and larger types can often be seen operating. The Great Northern Highway runs north through Bullsbrook, and passes the end of the runways.

This page has been intentionally left blank.

Sydney Kingsford Smith, Australia

SYD | YSSY

Tel: +61 2 9667 9111
Web: www.sydneyairport.com.au
Passengers: 32,998,000 (2008)

Overview

Australia's busiest airport, Sydney Kingsford Smith is very busy and often very sunny, making it a photographer's paradise. The location, in the suburb of Mascot and alongside Botany Bay, gives it numerous vantage points - more than the four mentioned in this guide.

Traffic comes from all corners of the globe, from local commuters and cargo aircraft to the largest jumbos. It is also the main base of Qantas, where they do their maintenance and bring most of their fleet through every week. Sydney has three main terminals, plus a freight area. The large International Terminal is full of amenities, plus an observation deck.

Spotting Locations

1. Domestic Terminal Windows

One of the better views of the action at Sydney is from the domestic terminal. You will need to pass through security to get to the windows, but don't need a boarding pass. The windows at the end of the pier look out over the domestic gates, runways, and the distant international terminal. So you won't miss many movements, and photography - albeit through glass - is acceptable.

2. International Terminal Observation Deck

The airport's official viewing area is atop the International Terminal. Views from here are good, covering most movements, and photography is possible with a good lens. The Sydney skyline is a nice backdrop to photos. There is a bar here serving food and drinks, through which you access the deck.

3. Beach

A very popular spot, the beach sits close to the International Terminal's aprons, and alongside runway 16R/34L. From the pleasant surroundings you can watch

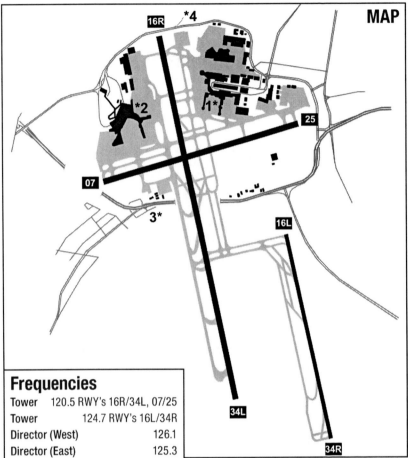

MAP

Frequencies

Tower	120.5	RWY's 16R/34L, 07/25
Tower	124.7	RWY's 16L/34R
Director (West)		126.1
Director (East)		125.3
Departures (South)		129.7
Departures (North)		123.0
Clearance Delivery		127.6
Clearance Delivery		133.8
Approach South		128.3
ATIS		112.1
ATIS		118.55
ATIS		126.25
Radar (North)		125.8
Radar (South)		124.55
Terminal		135.1
Approach (North)		124.4
Approach (West)		135.9
Departures (West)		118.4
Ground	121.7	E of RWY 16R/34L
Ground	126.5	W of RWY 16R/34

Runways

07/25   8,301ft / 2,530m
16L/34R 7,999ft / 2,438m
16R/34L 12,999ft / 3,962m

and photograph aircraft taxying and using the runway, and take some nice photographs. Some movements will be obscured, and you can't really see the terminals.

4. Qantas Drive

This spot is directly underneath the approach to runway 16R - so much that aircraft are very close to your head as they pass over. It is also good for runway 34L departures. You can also see movements using runway 16L/34R. To reach the spot from the International Terminal, head for the Domestic Terminals along Airport Drive, which turns into Qantas Drive. A grass area on the left allows parking, and views can be had from here, or by walking to get the correct angle.

Airlines

Aerolineas Argentinas
Aeropelican Air Services
Aircalin
Air Austral
Air Canada
Air China
Air Mauritius
Air New Zealand
Air Niugini
Air Pacific
Air Transport International
Air Vanuatu
Asiana Airlines
Atlas Air
Australian air Express
Brindabella Airlines
British Airways
Cathay Pacific
Cathay Pacific Cargo

China Airlines
China Eastern Airlines
China Southern Airlines
Delta Air Lines
DHL Express (Tasman Cargo Airlines)
Emirates
Etihad Airways
FedEx Express
Garuda Indonesia
Hainan Airlines
Hawaiian Airlines
Japan Airlines (JALways)
Jetstar
Korean Air
Korean Air Cargo
LAN Airlines
Malaysia Airlines
MASkargo

Norfolk Air (Our Airline)
Pacific Blue
Philippine Airlines
Polynesian Blue
Qantas
Qantas (Jetconnect)
Qantas (QantasLink)
Regional Express
Singapore Airlines
Singapore Airlines Cargo
Thai Airways International
Tiger Airways Australia
Toll Priority (Airwork)
United Airlines
UPS Airlines
V Australia
Vietnam Airlines
Virgin Atlantic Airways
Virgin Blue

Hotels

Stamford Plaza Hotel

O'Riordan/Robey Streets, Mascot NSW 2020 | +61 2 9317 2200 | www.stamford.com.au

The best hotel for spotting at Sydney. The Stamford Plaza has a rooftop pool area which overlooks the airport, and the AV8 bar offers views which non-guests can enjoy. Rooms 910-930 have distant views of the action.

Formule 1 Hotel

5 Ross Smith Ave, Mascot NSW 2020 | +61 2 8339 1840 | www.hotelformule1.com

Only certain rooms have views of any aircraft here, however the hotel is a great base for spotters at Sydney. It is located next to the GA area. The hotel is very affordable.

Nearby Attractions

Bankstown Airport

One of Sydney's other airport, which refers to itself as Sydney Metro, is Bankstown. This is a popular spot for enthusiasts as it is home to a number of stored historic aircraft at its southern side. The airfield itself is popular with GA and corporate flights, and it's possible to do a tour of the perimeter roads to see most aircraft. It is around 22 miles from Sydney Kingsford Smith Airport.

Australian Aviation Museum

Starkey Drive, Bankstown Airport, Panania NSW 2213 | +61 2 9791 3088 | www.aamb.com.au

Also located at Bankstown, this museum is home to a number of significant historic aircraft relevant to Australia. These include DC-3, de Havilland Dove and Heron and many more. Open 10am-4pam Saturday, Sunday and Wednesday. Adults $8, Under 15's $5, Concessions $6.

Airports in China & Taiwan

1. Beijing Capital International Airport
2. Beijing Nanyuan Airport
3. Chengdu Shuangliu International Airport
4. Dalian Zhoushuizi International Airport
5. Guangzhou Baiyun International Airport
6. Hangzhou Xiaoshan International Airport
7. Hong Kong Chek Lap Kok Airport
8. Kunming Wujiaba International Airport

9. Shanghai Hongqiao Airport
10. Shanghai Pudong International Airport
11. Shenzhen Bao'an International Airport
12. Taipei Songshan Airport
13. Taipei Taoyuan International Airport
14. Tianjin Binhai International Airport
15. Xiamen Gaoqi International Airport
16. Xi'an Xianyiang Airport

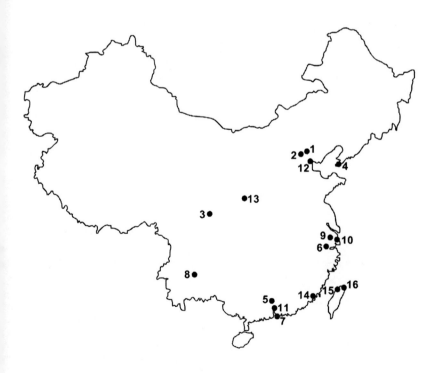

This page has been intentionally left blank.

Beijing Capital, China

PEK | ZBAA
Tel: +86 10 6454 1111
Web: www.bcia.com.cn
Passengers: 65,329,851 (2009)

Overview

The principal airport for Beijing, Capital has been steadily expanded and modernised and is today a large hub airport where domestic and international flights from all over the world meet. It is currently the world's second-busiest airport, and has three parallel runways, and a very large International Terminal to the east. The older domestic terminals and areas for maintenance and Chinese Air Force operations are to the north and west.

Capital is one of the better airports for spotting at in China, which is useful considering the sheer number of aircraft that pass through. It also has a good hotel for spotting.

A third airport for Beijing is due to be built and opened by 2015 to ease pressure on Capital. This will be at Daxing, to the south of the city.

The famous Datangshan museum is a short distance north of Capital Airport and well worth the visit for any airliner fans.

Spotting Locations

1. Viewing Mound

This dedicated area is situated under the final approach to runway 36R. It is elevated, with views over the western side of the airfield, Terminal 3, and the nearby executive apron. Photography is good from this spot, which is reached by walking along the twisting path from the terminal. Alternatively, you can reach the spot by road.

2. Domestic Terminals

Inside the Domestic Terminal you're free to roam around and enjoy the views from the windows. Photography is acceptable from here, and you can see across to the International Terminal. You should see all movements from this terminal.

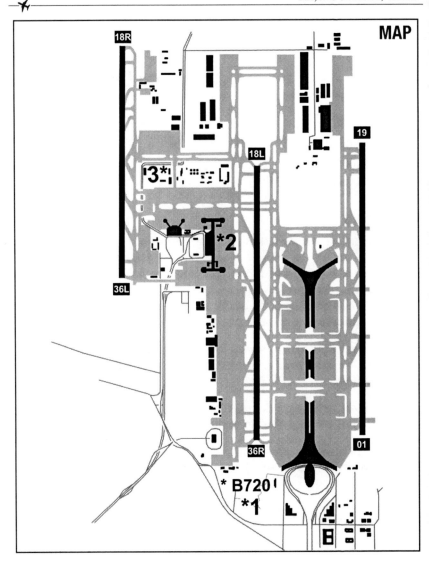

Frequencies

Tower	118.3
Tower	118.5
Ground	121.7
Delivery	121.6
Delivery	121.9
Approach	119.6
Approach	125.05
ATIS	127.6

Runways

1/19   12,468ft / 3,800m
18L/36R   12,468ft / 3,800m
18R/36L   10,499ft / 3,200m

3. Runway 18s

Walking about a mile north of the Domestic Terminals 1 and 2 takes you under the taxiways to an area between the runways 18L/R thresholds (albeit quite a distance apart). From here you can move about to monitor aircraft on these runways. You can also see aircraft parked on the remote and China Post service stands.

Airlines

Aeroflot
Aeroflot-Cargo
Aerosvit Airlines
Afriqiyah Airways
Air Algerie
Air Astana
Air Canada
Air China
Air China Cargo
Air France
Air Koryo
Air Macau
Air New Zealand
All Nippon Airways
All Nippon Airways
(Air Nippon)
Air Zimbabwe
AirBridgeCargo Airlines
American Airlines
Armavia
Asiana Airlines
Austrian Airlines
Beijing Capital Airlines
British Airways
Cargolux
Cathay Pacific
China Eastern Airlines
China Southern Airlines

Continental Airlines
Chongqing Airlines
Delta Air Lines
Dragonair
EgyptAir
El Al
Emirates
Ethiopian Airlines
Etihad Airways
Etihad Crystal Cargo
EVA Air
FedEx Express
Finnair
Garuda Indonesia
Grand China Air
Hainan Airlines
Hong Kong Airlines
Hong Kong Express
Airways
Iran Air
Japan Airlines
KLM
Korean Air
Korean Air Cargo
Lufthansa
Malaysia Airlines
MASkargo
MIAT Mongolian Airlines

Pakistan International
Airlines
Philippine Airlines
Qatar Airways
Rossiya
S7 Airlines
Scandinavian Airlines
Shandong Airlines
Shenzhen Airlines
Singapore Airlines
Singapore Airlines Cargo
Sichuan Airlines
SriLankan Airlines
TAAG Angola Airlines
Thai Airways International
Tianjin Airlines
Transaero Airlines
Turkmenistan Airlines
Turkish Airlines
United Airlines
Ural Airlines
Uzbekistan Airways
Vietnam Airlines
Vladivostok Air
Volga-Dnepr
Xiamen Airlines

Hotels

Citic Hotel Beijing Airport

Xiao Tianzhu Road, Capital International Airport, 100621 Beijing | +86 10 6456 5588 | www.
citichotelbeijing.com

The Citic (formerly the Sino Swiss) is located between the runways and has rooms facing either of 36L or 36R. Fire escapes on the corridors also have views of movements. Ask for rooms 707-711 or higher in the same range. There is also an area on the 11th floor that allows aircraft on the ground to be read with a good pole. The hotel is good value and less than 3 miles from the terminal, with a free shuttle bus.

Langham Place Hotel

1 Er Jing Road, Terminal 3, Capital International Airport, Beijing 100621 | +86 10 6457 5555
beijingairport.langhamplacehotels.com

An alternative to the Citic Hotel, the Langham Place is situated close to Terminal 3 and has rooms facing the runways, city skyline, or the lake. Rooms facing the runway look over the approach to runway 01, whilst those facing the lake will have views of aircraft approaching runway 36R, with 36L in the distance. It is not a particularly cheap hotel.

Nearby Attractions

Boeing 720

On the road passing the south-west side of the airport, there is a Boeing 720 (N7228U) parked just over the wall. Be quick or you'll miss it as the fence obscures it partially, and it is hidden amongst the buildings. See location marked on map.

China Aviation Museum (Datangshan)

Documentsnshan, Chan Ping County, Beijing | +86 10 6978 4882 | www.chn-am.com

Linked via a very long taxiway to Beijing Shahehzen airfield around 15 miles north east of Capital Airport. This excellent museum is a place all enthusiasts should visit once. It is home to a large number of airliner, transport and military aircraft in various states (many are fully preserved). These include HS121 Tridents, Ilyushin IL-18, Douglas DC-8, Vickers Viscount, many Lisunov Li-2's, MiG's, Shenyang F-5's and Ilyushin IL-10's. Over 200 aircraft can be found here. The museum is open daily from 8am to 5.30pm. Entrance is 40 Yuan for adults. Bus 912 runs from Andingmen Station to the gate of the museum.

Beijing Aviation Museum

37 Xueyuan Road, Haidian District, Beijing | +86 10 8231 7513

Turned into a museum in 1985, this large museum displays many different aircraft from Chinese aviation history. Although the vast majority of aircraft are military types, there are a few civil aircraft on display (military transport types). The museum is open Tuesday to Sunday, 8.30am-12pm and 2-5pm . The entrance fee is 4 Yuan.

Beijing Nanyuan Airport

(see separate entry)

Beijing Nanyuan, China

NAY | ZBNY

Passengers: 1,357,038 (2008)

Overview

Nanyuan is a mixed civil, military and government airport located close to the centre of Beijing. It is the oldest airport in China, having opened in 1910. Whilst Capital Airport is the primary airport for Beijing, Nanyuan is moderately busy as a domestic airport with sole operator China United Airlines.

The airport has a single runway and small passenger terminal. To the north and south of the passenger ramp are parking areas for government and military aircraft. Of note to the enthusiast are the Tupolev TU-154s used for official duties. They can often be seen parked up. Also of note is a small collection of preserved military aircraft (including transports) located just north of the passenger terminal, but armed guards often stand between you and the aircraft so it is not advised to stop.

With Nanyuan being a military airport, it is not advisable to try and take photographs around the terminal or the guards that can be found in most areas.

Spotting Locations

1. Passenger Terminal

You can read off any aircraft on the civil ramp from the passenger terminal's car park with ease, but beware of patroling guards. You cannot read off any movements from within the terminal.

2. Huang Yi Road

This road runs past the southern perimeter of the airport and passes the end of runway 36. A taxi driver should be able to find this easily for you. You can park in the field (not on the road) and read off the parked TU-154s and other aircraft on the southern aprons.

3. Northern Aprons

Driving (or walking) north from the terminal will pass the northern military apron. You can get fleeting glimpses of aircraft parked here through the tress.

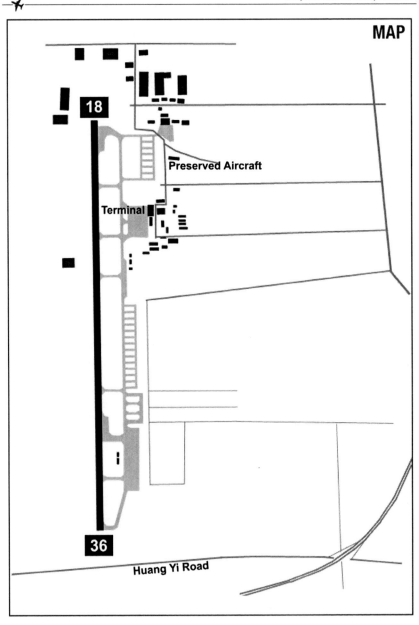

MAP

18

Preserved Aircraft

Terminal

36

Huang Yi Road

Frequencies
N/A

Runways
18/36   10,498ft / 3,200m

On your right is the collection of stored and preserved aircraft at the small museum. Guards are positioned around this area and will not allow you to stop or point cameras around.

Airlines

China United Airlines

Hotels

There are no hotels with views of aircraft movements near Nanyuan Airport. It would be better to stay at the hotels near Capital Airport.

Nearby Attractions

Beijing Capital Airport

(See separate entry)

This page has been intentionally left blank.

Chengdu Shuangliu International Airport, China

CTU | ZUUU

Tel: +86 28 8570 2649
Web: www.cdairport.com
Passengers: 22,637,762 (2009)

Overview

Chengdu is the busiest airport in western China, and one of the top ten busiest in the country with over 22 million passengers a year. It is also one of the country's busiest cargo airports.

The airport has recently opened a new parallel runway to the south of the existing one, giving more room for expansion and to handle the high numbers of movements. A new second terminal is also due to open in 2011, which is twice the size of the existing Terminal 1.

Spotting Locations

1. Terminal Cafés

Inside the terminal there are a couple of internet café's on the 2nd floor which have views over the apron. To be here you should buy food, drinks, or time on a computer. This can prove expensive, but there are no other landside views inside the terminal.

2. Runway 02L Track

A dirt track runs from the main at the southern end of the airport towards the security post close to the threshold of runway 02L. From here you can see aircraft landing on the runway, and taxiing towards the new runway. Security may move you on from here, but often spotters come to photograph aircraft at this spot and are left alone.

3. Runway 02L Fence

On the opposite side of the runway to the previous spot is an area of fence which can be reached by car. It offers views across the threshold and distant views to the parking aprons. Photography is good here for landing traffic, and aircraft lining up. The road to reach this spot is reached by following the main road leading to the previous spot, but carrying on and taking the next right after joining the bigger road. At the end, turn right again.

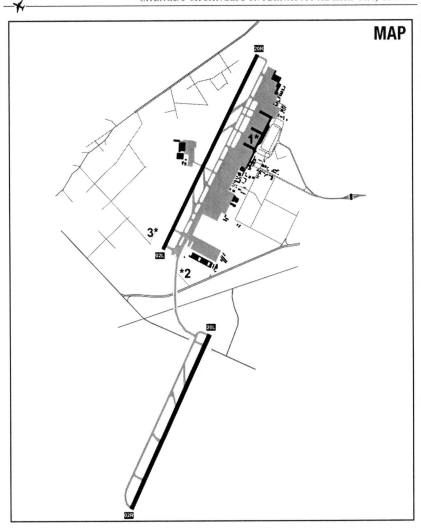

MAP

Frequencies

Tower	118.85
Tower	123.0
Ground	121.85
Approach	120.2
Approach	125.6
ATIS	128.6

Runways

2L/20R	11,811ft / 3,600m
2R/20L	11,811ft / 3,600m

Airlines

Air China
Air China Cargo
Air Macau
AirAsia X
Asiana Airlines
Beijing Capital Airlines
China Airlines
China Eastern Airlines
China Southern Airlines
China United Airlines
Dragonair
Hainan Airlines
Jade Cargo International
Juneyao Airlines
KLM
Lucky Air
Okay Airlines
Shandong Airlines
Shenzhen Airlines
Sichuan Airlines
SilkAir
Spring Airlines
Thai Airways International
TransAsia Airways
United Eagle Airlines
Xiamen Airlines

Hotels

Chengdu Airport Hotel

Shuangliu, Chengdu Airport | +86 28 8520 5577

A very basic 2-star hotel very conveniently located just south of Terminal 1. There are no known views of movements from here, but you can quickly walk to the terminal.

Nearby Attractions

Taipingsi Airfield

Taipingsi is a military and government airfield only four miles east of Chengdu Shuangliu. It is not very busy, but occasionally handles government transport aircraft, and a fleet of air force helicopters. The airfield occupies a large open space, and you can get a distant view to the aprons from the opposite side.

Chiang Airfield

Chiang is an air force base around 9 miles north of Shuangliu. It is quite active with fighter jet movements from its single runway. The best locations to watch movements are from the various roads around the perimeter.

Chengdu-Feng Huang Shan Airfield

Another military airfield to the north of the city. It is home to the 2nd Army Aviation Regiment's helicopter fleets. You can get fleeting views of the ramps from the roads surrounding the airfield. Security can be tight.

Dalian Zhoushuizi International Airport, China

DLC | ZYTL

Tel: +86 411 8388 6699
Web: www.dlairport.com
Passengers: 7,281,084 (2007)

Overview

Dalian Zhoushuizi is a joint civil-military airport in the north east of China. The airport is on the route network of most Chinese carriers, and those from nearby North and South Korea, Russia and Japan. It has a modern terminal building and a single runway. The airport is closely surrounded by the city, giving little room for expansion.

Because of the military presence, photography of aircraft is not permitted and security guards will pay you a visit if spotted.

Spotting Locations

1. Runway 10

A road runs through the industrial and residential area to the west of the terminal building. Various areas of waste ground can be used to get views of aircraft on the taxiway and runway.

2. Runway 28

It is possible to get views of aircraft approaching and lining up on runway 28 from areas of waste ground either side of the main road running down the eastern perimeter. Be careful not to cause an obstruction.

Airlines

Air China
Air Koryo
All Nippon Airways
Asiana Airlines
China Eastern Airlines
China Express Airlines

MAP

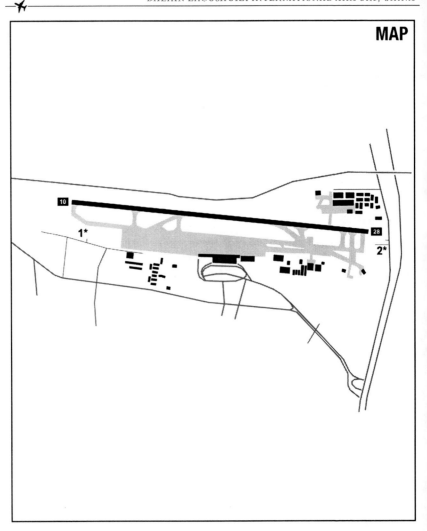

Frequencies

Tower	118.25
Tower	118.85
Approach	123.85
Approach	127.95
ATIS	126.65

Runways

10/28 10,827ft / 3,300m

China Southern Airlines
China West Air
Grand China Air
Grand China Express
Hainan Airlines
Japan Airlines
Juneyao Airlines
Korean Air
Okay Airlines
SAT Airlines
Shandong Airlines
Shanghai Airlines
Shenzhen Airlines
Sichuan Airlines
Spring Airlines
TransAsia Airways
UNI Air
United Eagle Airlines
Xiamen Airlines

Hotels

Dalian International Airport Hotel

539 Changjiang Road, Zhoushuizi 116011 | +86 411 8252 9999

This airport is actually quite a distance from the terminal - over a mile along the main access road. As such no views of movements can be had from its rooms. Nevertheless it is a clean, modern hotel and convenient for travellers.

Nearby Attractions

Dalian Tuchengzi Air Base

A fairly large air base situated around 20 miles west of Dalian. It is home to a bomber squadron and usually has some military transport aircraft on the ground. It is not possible to get any views on the ground, but aircraft approaching from the east will pass over the main road through Jiangjia.

This page has been intentionally left blank.

Guangzhou Baiyun International Airport, China

CAN | ZGGG

Web: www.baiyunairport.com/english/
Passengers: 37,048,550 (2009)

Overview

Guangzhou Baiyun International opened in August 2004, replacing the previous airport of the same name which had outgrown its crowded city location. The new airport has two parallel runways and a large central terminal complex with four piers. Already, plans are underfoot to expand the airport with another parallel runway and second terminal.

Guangzhou is now China's second-busiest airport, handling almost 40 million passengers per year. Also, since 2008 the airport has been the Asia-Pacific hub for FedEx Express and handles around 140 flights per week from the dedicated cargo complex to the north of the terminal.

Spotting Locations

1. Terminals

Inside the terminals there are plenty of windows through which parked aircraft and movements can be observed. However, the number of aircraft that can be seen is limited to whichever side of the terminal you are in. Many of the windows are restricted to those with boarding passes.

2. Runway 2L

The corner of a service road a short walk south of the terminal offers views over the taxiway and runway 2L threshold. It is good for photography but has limited views of traffic on the opposite runway.

3. Runway 2R

On the opposite side, another service road leads to a point alongside the threshold of runway 2R and associated taxiways. These two locations are around 1.5 miles from the terminal.

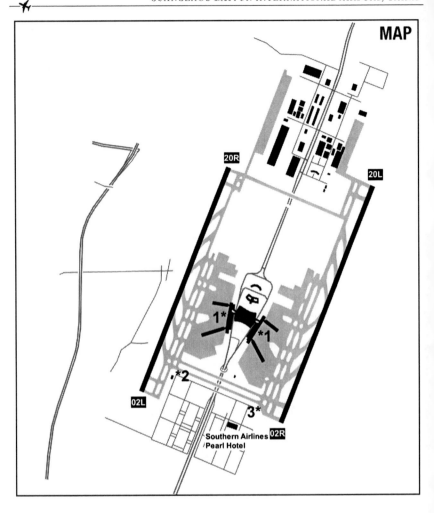

Frequencies

Tower	118.1
Tower	118.8
Tower	124.3
Ground	121.75
Ground	121.85
Ground	121.6
Clearance Delivery	121.95
Approach	120.4
Approach	126.35
Approach	119.6
Approach	119.7
ATIS	128.6

Runways

2L/20R 11,811ft / 3,600m
2R/20L 12,467ft / 3,800m
TBA 12,467ft / 3,800m (Under Construction)

Airlines

Air China	Hainan Airlines
Air France	Japan Airlines
Air Madagascar	Kenya Airways
AirAsia	Korean Air
All Nippon Airways	Korean Air Cargo
Asiana Airlines	Kunpeng Airlines
Asiana Cargo	Lufthansa
Batavia Air	Lufthansa Cargo
Cebu Pacific	Malaysia Airlines
China Airlines	MASkargo
China Airlines Cargo	Qatar Airways
China Eastern Airlines	Saudi Arabian Airlines
China Postal Airlines	Shandong Airlines
China Southern Airlines	Shanghai Airlines
China Southern Cargo	Shenzhen Airlines
China United Airlines	Sichuan Airlines
China West Air	Singapore Airlines
Deer Air	Spring Airlines
Delta Air Lines	SriLankan Airlines
Dragonair	Thai AirAsia
EgyptAir	Thai Airways International
Emirates	Tiger Airways
Ethiopian Airlines	United Eagle Airlines
Etihad Crystal Cargo	UPS Airlines
EVA Air	Vietnam Airlines
EVA Air Cargo	Xiamen Airlines
FedEx Express	Yangtze River Express
Garuda Indonesia	Yemenia

Hotels

Southern Airlines Pearl Hotel

Air Harbor Five Road, Southern Workaround, New Baiyun International Airport, Guangzhou
+86 40 0818 6868 | www.cs-airhotel.com

Located very close to the airport, this is a smart European-style hotel. High rooms facing
the airport have views of most movements, but you'll need a SBS after dark, or walk a
short distance to an overpass from which you can read movements.

Nearby Attractions

Civil Aviation College

The old airport's college site has now largely been transported to this new site near the new airport. It is home to a number of aircraft including three Hawker Siddeley Tridents and two Ilyushin IL-14's. Taxi drivers will be happy to take you here and help you see what you need to.

Hangzhou Xiaoshan International Airport, China

HGH | ZSHC

Web: www.hzairport.com
Passengers: 14,944,716 (2009)

Overview

Hangzhou is a relatively new airport, with construction only starting in 1997 and the airport opening in 2000. It was built to replace the joint civil-military airport nearby, and is already being expanded to cope with growing demand. Air China now has a hub operation here, and there is a decent size cargo operation from the ramp to the south-west of the terminal.

Spotting Locations

1. Terminal Windows

The windows in the departures area of the terminal are good for photography. Some movements will be missed depending on which part of the terminal you are in, but walking around gives you more opportunities to note aircraft.

2. Runway 07

Heading towards the city away from the terminal, side roads lead off the motorway (you can pass underneath) and south through a couple of villages. Follow the small roads shown on the map and you'll come to the end of runway 07, from where excellent photos can be taken of aircraft on approach. Not much else can be seen, however.

Airlines

Air China	China United Airlines	Okay Airways
Air China Cargo	Deer Air	Shandong Airlines
Air Macau	EVA Air	Shanghai Airlines
Air Nippon	Grand China Express Air	Shenzhen Airlines
AirAsia X	Hainan Airlines	Spring Airlines
Asiana Airlines	Hong Kong Airlines	Sichuan Airlines
Chengdu Airlines	KLM	TransAsia Airways
China Eastern Airlines	Korean Air Cargo	UNI Air
China Southern Airlines	Mandarin Airlines	Xiamen Airlines

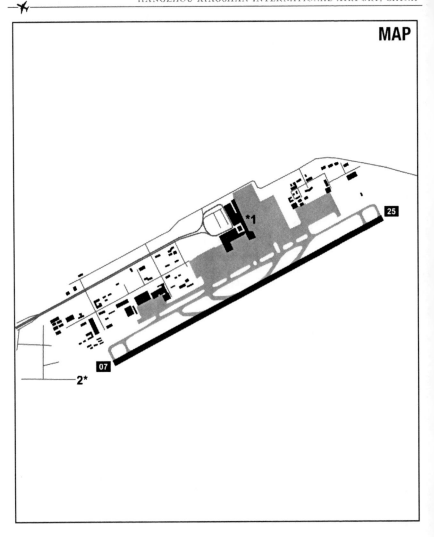

MAP

Frequencies

Tower	118.3
Tower	130.0
Ground	121.75
Approach	119.15
Approach	126.05
ATIS	127.25

Runways

7/25   11,811ft / 3,600m

Hotels

There are no hotels in the immediate vicinity of the airport, and therefore none with views of aircraft. There are plenty of hotels in Hangzhou city.

Nearby Attractions

Hangzhou Air Base

Situated north west of the city centre, this was the former joint civil-military airport at Hangzhou. It is still used for military operations.

This page has been intentionally left blank.

Hong Kong Chek Lap Kok, China

HKG | VHHH

Tel: +852 2181 8888
Web: http://www.hongkongairport.com/eng/
Passengers: 46,167,000 (2009)

Overview

Opened in 1998, Chek Lap Kok replaced the legendary Kai Tak airport in Kowloon Bay, which was always a draw to aviation enthusiasts due to its interesting approach and nice mix of airliners. The mix is still here, but the new airport is much more spacious and modern, with two runways and a large central terminal complex. The cargo apron is on the southern side, whilst Cathay Pacific's maintenance base is on the western side of the airport. Hong Kong is always busy and a pleasure to spot at.

Spotting Locations

1. Viewing Deck

This official location is on top of Terminal 2. It is accessed via the Aviation Discovery Centre, and you require a ticket to enter (bought from the cinema entrance). This is a good location for an overall view of movements, and you won't really miss anything going on at the airport. It is good for photographing arrivals on runway 25R, although aircraft on the ground can be too distant. The deck is open daily from 10.30am-10pm.

2. Maintenance Areas

At the extreme western side of the airport, there are a number of locations near the maintenance hangars which are great for watching and photographing arrivals and departures. You can also log aircraft parked in this area. It is a long walk from the terminals, so take a car or the S52 bus (destination Aircraft Maintenance Area) from Tung Chung. The S1 bus runs from the terminal to Tung Chung.

3. Inside Terminal

Once airside in the terminal, there are plenty of windows in all gate areas. This gives you plenty of opportunity to log aircraft coming and going, and to watch arrivals on the runways. However, given the size of the terminal it can become a difficult slog to cover all areas, even with the use of the shuttle train. Photography is also through glass, so not perfect.

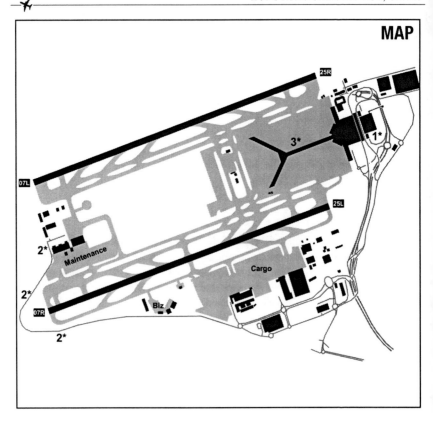

MAP

Frequencies

Tower	118.2
Tower	118.4
Tower	118.7
Ground	121.6
Ground	122.55
Precision	133.7
Clearance Delivery	124.65
Clearance Delivery	129.9
Departure	123.8
Departure	124.05
Approach	119.1
Approach	119.35
Approach	133.7
Zone Control	120.6
Flight Service	121.0
Flight Service	122.4
ATIS	128.2

Runways

07R/25L	12,467ft / 3,800m
07L/25R	12,467ft / 3,800m

Airlines

ACT Airlines
Aeroflot
Aeroflot-Cargo
Aerologic
Air Atlanta Icelandic
Air Canada
Air Cargo Germany
Air China
Air China Cargo
Air France
Air France Cargo
Air Hong Kong
Air India
Air Mauritius
Air Mauritius Cargo
Air New Zealand
Air Niugini
Air Pacific
AirAsia
AirBridgeCargo Airlines
All Nippon Airways
All Nippon Airways
(Air Japan)
ANA Cargo
Aryan Cargo Express
Asiana Airlines
Asiana Cargo
Atlas Air
Avient Aviation
Bangkok Airways
Biman Bangladesh
Airlines
British Airways
British Airways
World Cargo
Cargoitalia
Cargolux
Cargolux Italia
Cathay Pacific
Cathay Pacific Cargo
Cebu Pacific
China Airlines

China Airlines Cargo
China Eastern Airlines
China Southern Airlines
Continental Airlines
Continental Micronesia
Deccan 360
Delta Air Lines
DETA Air
DHL Air UK
Donghai Airlines
Dragonair
Dragonair Cargo
El Al
El Al Cargo
Emirates
Emirates SkyCargo
Ethiopian Airlines
Ethiopian Airlines Cargo
Etihad Crystal Cargo
EVA Air
EVA Air Cargo
Evergreen International
Airlines
FedEx Express
Finnair
Finnair Cargo
Garuda Indonesia
Grandstar Cargo
Hong Kong Airlines
Hong Kong Airlines Cargo
Hong Kong Express
Jade Cargo International
Japan Airlines
Jeju Air
Jetstar Asia Airways
Jett8 Airlines Cargo
Jet Airways
Kalitta Air
Kenya Airways
Kingfisher Airlines
KLM
KLM Cargo

Korean Air
Korean Air Cargo
Lufthansa
Lufthansa Cargo
Malaysia Airlines
Mandala Airlines
Mandarin Airlines
Martinair Cargo
MASkargo
Midex Airlines
MNG Airlines Cargo
Nepal Airlines
Nippon Cargo Airlines
Orient Thai Airlines
Pakistan International
Airlines
Philippine Airlines
Philipping Airlines Cargo
Polar Air Cargo
Polet Airlines
Qantas
Qatar Airways
Qatar Airways Cargo
Royal Brunei Airlines
Royal Jordanian
Saudi Arabian Airlines
Saudi Arabian
Airlines Cargo
Shanghai Airlines
Shenzhen Airlines
Sichuan Airlines
Singapore Airlines
Singapore Airlines Cargo
South African Airways
Southern Air
Spring Airlines
SriLankan Airlines
Star Airlines Macedonia
Swiss International
Air Lines
Thai AirAsia
Thai Airway International

Tiger Airways
TNT Airways
Transmile Air Services
Tri-MG Intra Asia Airlines
Turkish Airlines

Turkish Cargo
ULS Cargo
United Airlines
UPS Airlines
Vietnam Airlines

Virgin Atlantic Airways
World Airways
Xiamen Airlines
Yangtze River Express

Hotels

Regal Airport Hotel

9 Cheong Tat Road, Hong Kong International Airport, Hong Kong | +825 2276 8888
www.regalhotel.com

This hotel is linked to the terminal building and some rooms have excellent views of aircraft. Be sure to ask for a room with views of the airport, and higher up if possible. The hotel is very expensive, but is comfortable and has the benefit of the views and a restaurant which also overlooks the aprons and runways.

Marriott Skycity Hotel

1 SkyCity Road East, Hong Kong International Airport, Lantau Hong Kong | +852 3969 1888
www.marriott.com

Rooms in this hotel offer excellent views, and it's only a short walk from the terminal and its Skydeck viewing area. Even numbered rooms high up offer views of short finals to runway 07R, and some views of the cargo ramp. An SBS would be useful for night movements.

Nearby Attractions

Douglas DC-3

A preserved Cathay Pacific DC-3 is present in the airport's Cathay City area with fictitious registration VR-HDA (real registration RP-C1101, cn 9525). It is visible from the A10 and S52 buses.

Kai Tak Airport

Although no aircraft remain on site, the old Kai Tak Airport can still be made out in places - particularly the old runway which juts out into Kowloon Bay on its own peninsula. Construction work is happening at a very fast rate, however, so it is only a matter of time before nothing remains of the old airport.

Shenzhen Airport

(see separate entry)

Kunming Wujiaba International Airport, China

KMG | ZPPP
Web: www.ynairport.com
Passengers: 18,944,716 (2009)

Overview

Kunming Wujiaba Airport is one of the few big airports in China still located in a relatively downtown location. It is bursting at the seams, with around 19 million passengers per year making it the 7th busiest in the country. It has a single runway and a lot of aircraft have to park on remote stands.

Due to the conditions here, a completely new airport is due to open in 2012. It will be named Zheng He International Airport, and will be located around 15 miles north east of the city. The existing airport is to be demolished once the new one opens.

Spotting Locations

1. Guanyu Road

This road passes the end of runway 21 and has an elevated view which is good for photographing aircraft on approach and seeing some movements on the ground. There are shops nearby and the road is busy, but spotters can often be found here. It is quite far to walk from the terminal.

2. Terminal

The windows in the central terminal area and pier look out over most gates and the runway, but are not very good for photographs. You will see all movements from the terminal.

Airlines

Air China	Dragonair
Beijing Capital Airlines	EVA Air
Chengdu Airlines	Hainan Airlines
China Eastern Airlines	Hong Kong Airlines
China Southern Airlines	Juneyao Airlines
China West Air	Korean Air

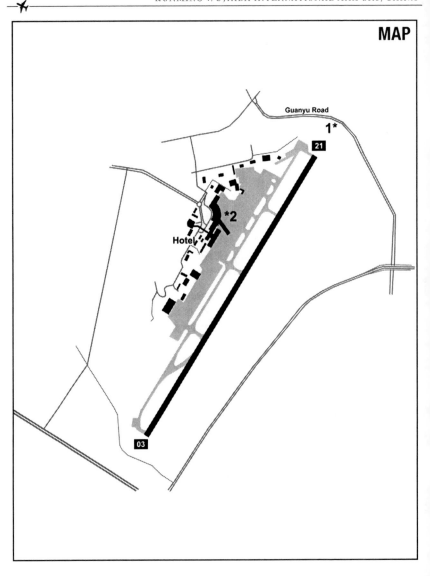

MAP

Guanyu Road

1*

21

*2

Hotel

03

Frequencies

Tower	118.1
Tower	118.85
Ground	121.65
Ground	121.85
Approach	124.25
Approach	127.9
ATIS	128.45

Runways

3/21   11,155ft / 3,400m

Kunming Airlines	Sichuan Airlines
Lao Airlines	SilkAir
Lucky Air	Spring Airlines
Malaysia Airlines	Thai Airways International
Okay Airlines	TransAsia Airways
Shandong Airlines	UNI Air
Shanghai Airlines	Vietnam Airlines
Shenzhen Airlines	Xiamen Airlines

Hotels

Kunming Airport Hotel

Wujiaba International Airport, Kunming 650200 | +86 871 711 3120

Conveniently located just outside the terminal and with affordable, clean rooms. Few rooms, if any, offer views of movements.

Nearby Attractions

Shorts Belfast 03

Across the bay to the south west of Wujiaba Airport is a preserved Shorts Belfast aircraft, serial '03'. It is situated alongside the X014 road in a compound, around a 13 mile drive.

This page has been intentionally left blank.

Shanghai Hongqiao, China

SHA | ZSSS

Tel: +86 21 96990
Web: www.shairport.com/eng/
Passengers: 25,078,548 (2009)

Overview

Hongqiao was Shanghai's main airport until 1999 when the new Pudong Airport to the east of the city opened, relieving some of the strain. Despite this, Hongqiao remains the fourth busiest airport in China and is a lot closer to the city centre. It is mainly a domestic airport, although some international flights operate. Hongqiao is also a busy cargo airport.

For spotters, it is good to spend time at both Shanghai airports to make sure you catch aircraft that don't operate from both. Hongqiao authorities unfortunately closed its dedicated viewing area only a short while after opening.

Spotting Locations

1. Observation Deck

This viewing area was opened in March 2010 on top of Terminal 2, hopefully paving the way for more such areas to be provided across the country. The area can be found on the fourth floor of the building and has a security check on entry. It offers excellent views over the apron and runways. Photography is good, also. Unfortunately the viewing deck has been closed since shortly after opening and it is unknown whether it will re-open. There is a canteen area alongside the observation deck's entrance which can be used, however.

2. Terminal 2 Access Roads

The roads leading up to Terminal 2 offer numerous opportunities for viewing aircraft parked on the ground and using the runways. You may be moved on if security come across you, but many spotters have found these elevated roads useful.

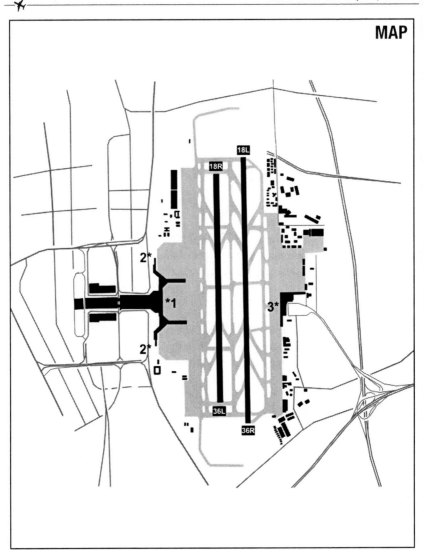

MAP

Frequencies

Tower	118.1
Tower	124.3
Ground	118.1
Ground	121.6
Clearance Delivery	121.75
Approach	119.75
Approach	120.8
ATIS	132.25

Runways

18L/36R	11,154ft / 3,400m
18R/36L	10,827ft / 3,300m

3. Terminal 1

The windows in the domestic Terminal 1 are great for viewing traffic and photographing aircraft parked close to you. You will not see much at the distant Terminal 2 from here, but aircraft on the runway are visible if you pick your spot.

Airlines

Air China	Hong Kong Airlines
All Nippon Airways	Japan Airlines
Asiana Airlines	Juneyao Airlines
China Airlines	Korean Air
China Eastern Airlines	Shandong Airlines
China Southern Airlines	Shanghai Airlines
China United Airlines	Shenzhen Airlines
Dragonair	Sichuan Airlines
EVA Air	Spring Airlines
Grand China Express	TransAsia Airways
Hainan Airlines	Xiamen Airlines
Hebei Airlines	

Hotels

Hong Gang Shanghai Hotel

2550 Hongqiao Road, Shanghai 200335 | +86 21 6268 1008

Ask for a high room with number ending in 10 - 910 for example is a good room. Others include 606 and 702. These all face the terminal's parking ramps and are perfect for spotting and photography. The hotel is very reasonably priced.

Argyle Hotel

458 Hong Gang Yi Lu, Changning District, Shanghai | +86 21 6268 7788 | www.argylehotels.com

Has rooms facing the runways at Honqiao, so offers some good views. Ask for rooms in these ranges for the best views: 817-820, 917-920. Photography is possible from the rooms, and prices are reasonable.

Nearby Attractions

Shanghai Pudong Airport

(see separate entry)

This page has been intentionally left blank.

Shanghai Pudong International Airport, China

PVG | ZSPD

Tel: +86 21 96990
Web: www.shairport.com/eng/
Passengers: 31,900,000 (2009)

Overview

Pudong International is one of Asia's busiest airports. It was opened in 1999, replacing the existing Hongqiao Airport which was no longer able to expand. Pudong is situated around 20 miles east of the city, and currently has three parallel runways and two passenger terminals; it is also a large cargo hub with various ramps on either side of the airport dedicated to this.

Unfortunately Pudong wasn't built with the enthusiast in mind. Unlike Hongqiao, no dedicated viewing facilities are provided, and very few views through terminal windows are possible without going through security. What's more, the roads around the airport do not offer many views. Because of this, many spotters have better luck by booking a room in one of the airport hotels which overlooks the action.

Buses run to Hongqiao Airport from Pudong on a regular basis from outside domestic arrivals. It is useful to visit both airports as many aircraft in the fleets of the bigger carriers do not visit both.

Spotting Locations

1. International Terminal

There is a windows in the terminal with some views of aircraft on the international side of the airport. Head up to departures level and walk to the end alongside the coffee shop. Be discrete as some security officers like to move spotters on.

2. Southerly Arrivals

If aircraft are arriving on the 35L/R runways, you can walk south from the terminal along the road and find a spot which has views. Photography isn't very good from this area, but at least you can log most arrivals.

MAP

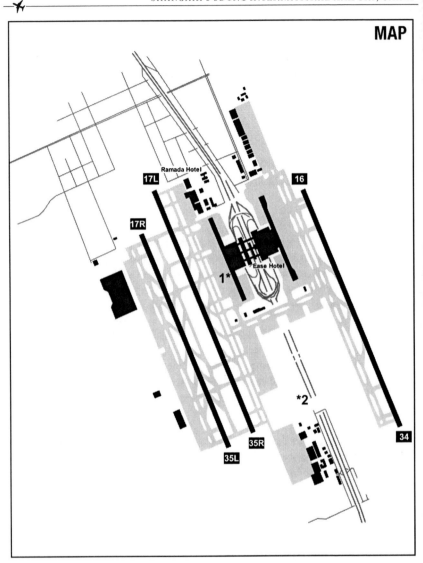

Frequencies

Tower East	118.4
Tower East	124.35
Ground East	121.7
Ground East	121.8
Clearance Delivery	121.95
Approach	119.75
Approach	120.8
ATIS	127.85

Runways

16/34   12,467ft / 3,800m
17L/35R   13,123ft / 4,000m
17R/35L   11,154ft / 3,400m

Airlines

Aeroflot
Aeroflot-Cargo
Aeromexico
Air Canada
Air China
Air China Cargo
Air France
Air Hong Kong
Air India
Air Koryo
Air Macau
Air New Zealand
AirBridgeCargo Airlines
All Nippon Airways
American Airlines
ANA & JP Express
Asiana Airlines
Atlas Air
British Airways
Cargolux
Cathay Pacific
Cebu Pacific
China Airlines
China Cargo Airlines
China Eastern Airlines
China Southern Airlines
China Southern Cargo
Continental Airlines

Delta Air Lines
Dragonair
Emirates
Emirates SkyCargo
Etihad Crystal Cargo
EVA Air
EVA Air Cargo
FedEx Express
Finnair
Garuda Indonesia
Grand China Express
Great Wall Airlines
Hainan Airlines
Hong Kong Airlines
Hong Kong Express
Airways
Japan Airlines
Japan Airlines
(JAL Express)
Juneyao Airlines
KLM
Korean Air
Lufthansa
Malaysia Airlines
Martinair Cargo
MASkargo
Nippon Cargo Airlines
Philippine Airlines

Polar Air Cargo
Qantas
Qatar Airways
Royal Brunei Airlines
Saudi Arabian
Airlines Cargo
Shandong Airlines
Shanghai Airlines
Shanghai Airlines Cargo
Shenzhen Airlines
Sichuan Airlines
Singapore Airlines
Singapore Airlines Cargo
Spring Airlines
SriLankan Airlines
Swiss International
Air Lines
Thai Airways International
TNT Airways
Transasia Airways
Turkish Airlines
United Airlines
UPS Airlines
Vietnam Airlines
Virgin Atlantic Airways
Volga-Dnepr
Xiamen Airlines

Hotels

Dazhong Merrylin 'Ease' Hotel Pudong Airport

6001 Yingbin Avenue, Pudong New Area, Shanghai 201202 | +86 21 3879 9999
www.motel168.com

This hotel is reasonably priced and has a direct link to the terminal and train station. Rooms on higher floors facing south have views over the taxiways and runways. An SBS is useful for night-time movements.

Ramada Pudong Airport Shanghai

1100 Qi Hang Road, Shanghai 201207 | +86 21 3849 4949 | www.ramada.com

This hotel is also reasonably priced, but offers much fewer opportunities. Again, ask for a south facing room looking towards the airport, and on a high floor. You will then get distant views of runway movements and terminal views.

Nearby Attractions

Shanghai Aviation Enthusiast Centre

This place has a DC-8, IL-14, and MiG helicopters on display and open to the public. It is quite difficult to get to. You must take Shanghai Metro line 1 to Jin Jiang Park station, then walk to the left along Humin Rd. Pass through the underpass, emerging next to the fair ground. Then continue walking down the road until you reach the centre on your left. There is a very small entrance fee.

Shanghai Hongqiao Airport

(see separate entry)

Shenzhen Bao'an International, China

SZX | ZGSZ

Tel: +86 755 2345 6789
Web: www.szairport.com
Passengers: 24,486,406 (2009)

Overview

China's fourth busiest airport, Shenzhen Bao'an has grown massively in importance. So much so that it is developing a huge new terminal and second runway parallel to the existing runway 15/33. These expansions are due to open in 2012 and see the airport's capacity increased.

Since the city of Shenzhen is a big manufacturing base, the airport handles a lot of cargo flights in addition to the large range of passenger airlines with flights across China and the rest of the Far East.

Spotting Locations

1. Runway 33 River Embankment

At the southern end of the airport, a track runs alongside the river embankment which passes the end of runway 33. This leads to the construction area for the new terminal and runway. It offers some good positions to photograph and watch aircraft on approach and lining up. Signs warn of robbers, but there are usually only friendly fishermen around.

2. Runway 15/Ferry Terminal

At the northern end of the airport is the Fujun Ferry Terminal with services to Hong Kong and Macau. From the road running past the terminal you can get views of aircraft on approach to runway 15 and lining up for takeoff.

3. Terminal Drive

The road running between the terminals offers some good elevated views over various parking stands from which you can note down aircraft and take pictures.

MAP

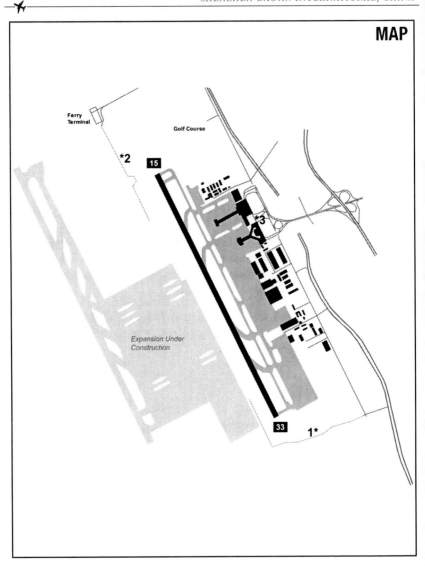

Frequencies

Tower 118.05
Tower 118.45
Ground 121.65
Ground 121.875
Clearance Delivery 127.95
Approach 120.35
Approach 124.25
ATIS 127.45

Runways

15/33   11,155ft / 3,400m

Airlines

AirAsia

Air China

Asiana Airlines

Chengdu Airlines

China Airlines

China Eastern Airlines

China Southern Airlines

EVA Air

FedEx Express

Hainan Airlines

Jade Cargo International

Juneyao Airlines

Korean Air

Kunming Airlines

Shanghai Airlines

Shandong Airlines

Shenzhen Airlines

Shenzhen Donghai Airlines

Sichuan Airlines

SilkAir

Spring Airlines

Sky Shuttle

Thai AirAsia

Tiger Airways

TNT Airways

Transmile Air Services

UNI Air

UPS Airlines

Xiamen Airlines

Yangtze River Express

Hotels

Sunway Airport Hotel

Bao An District, Shenzhen International Airport Guangdong 518128 | +86 21 6322 3855

This hotel has somewhat distant views of the airport. Ask for a high, even numbered room facing the airport. You'll need good binoculars or an SBS. The hotel is very reasonably priced, and has an excellent sports bar and coffee shop.

Nearby Attractions

Hong Kong Chek Lap Kok

(see separate entry)

This page has been intentionally left blank.

Taipei Songshan, Taiwan

TSA | RCSS

Passengers: 4,470,859 (2007)

Overview

Originally Taipei's main international airport, Songshan was superseded by the new Taoyuan Airport in 1979. Songshan had become overcrowded and unable to cope with traffic levels or growth. Since then it has been relegated to the role of the city's domestic airport. However, flights do operate to some international destinations, including Japan and mainland China.

Songshan is located close to the city centre. It has a single runway and terminal, with areas for use by the Republic of China Air Force. Because of this military presence, photography is officially banned at the airport, so bear this in mind when spotting.

There have been talks to close Songshan in favour of developing the prime location and because high speed rail travel has now take a large chunk out of the domestic flight market. However, for the time being these plans have been put on hold and in fact the airport has been undergoing modernisation to bring its facilities up to date.

Spotting Locations

1. Runway 10

The road running past the end of runway 10 is a great place to stop and watch aircraft - particularly if they are arriving on this runway. You can stand on higher ground alongside the road where you'll often find other spotters congregating. From here you have a good view of aircraft taxiing to the runway and landing. It is good for photographs too. It takes around 20 minutes to walk to this point from the terminal.

2. Terminal Windows

You can walk through to the various windows inside the terminal and see most movements on the runway and remote ramps. Remember that photography is not permitted, and you will be questioned by security if spotted using a camera.

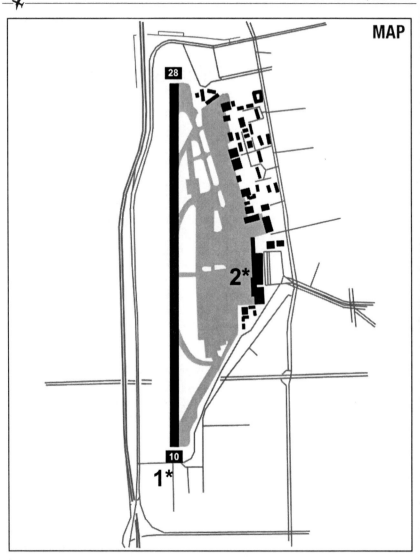

Frequencies

Tower	118.1
Tower	126.3
Ground	121.9
Clearance Delivery	121.2
Approach	119.6
Approach	119.7
Approach	123.5
ATIS	127.4

Runways

10/28 8,547ft / 2,605m

Airlines

Air China
All Nippon Airways
China Airlines
China Eastern Airlines
EVA Air
Japan Airlines
Mandarin Airlines
Shanghai Airlines
Sichuan Airlines
TransAsia Airways
UNI Air
Xiamen Airlines

Hotels

Riviera Taipei

646 Linsen N. Road, Taipei 104 | +886 2 2585 3258 | www.rivierataipei.com

Fairly close to the end of runway 10 at Songshan, the Riviera is the closest you'll get to a spotting hotel here. Higher rooms facing the airport allow aircraft to be read off on approach and lining up on the runway. It is also a only a short walk from spotting location 1.

Nearby Attractions

Taipei Taoyuan Airport

(see separate entry)

This page has been intentionally left blank.

Taipei Taoyuan International Airport, Taiwan

TPE | RCTP

Web: www.taoyuanairport.gov.tw

Passengers: 21,616,729 (2009)

Overview

The busiest and largest airport in Taiwan, Taoyuan International (formerly known as Chiang Kai-shek) was opened in 1979 to allow expansion in the country's air services over the crowded Songshan Airport in the city centre. Taoyuan itself is around 20 miles east of the city.

The airport is very busy, with an extensive mix of airlines from Asia, North America and Europe visiting regularly. It is also one of the world's busiest cargo airports, and many cargo airlines pass through every day. In particular, it is a hub for China Airlines Cargo and EVA Air Cargo.

There are two parallel runways and two passenger terminals at Taoyuan. Terminal 1 has recently undergone an extensive renovation project. Terminal 3 is expected to open by 2014.

Located just south of the airport is Taoyuan Air Base.

Spotting Locations

1. South Crash Gate

Where a rough taxiway links Taoyuan Airport with Taoyuan Air Base, a crash gate can be found in the fence alongside runway 06/24. You can drive, or walk if blocked, along the taxiway to the gate from the main road which runs between the airport and base. When heading away from the terminal, take the first left off the motorway and follow along. From here you'll have a good vantage point of aircraft on the runway, and it's possible to take good photographs. Other spotters congregate here.

2. "Miracle" Cafe

On the north side of the airfield is a cafe dubbed the "Miracle" Cafe due to the face it narrowly escaped damage when an Airbus A300 crashed alongside. It has views over the northern side of the airfield, and from its rooftop you can take acceptable photographs from afternoon till sunset. The cafe is situated on the main '15' road running along the northern perimeter.

MAP

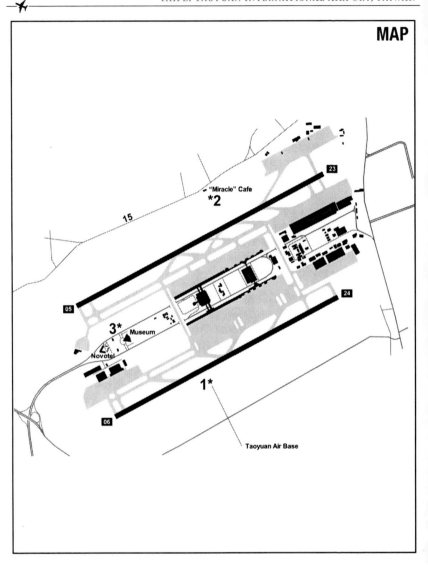

Frequencies

Tower	118.7
Tower 129.3	
Ground	121.7
Clearance Delivery 121.8	
Approach	119.6
Approach	119.7
Approach	125.1
ATIS 127.6	

Runways

6/24	10,991ft / 3,350m
5/23	12,008ft / 3,660m

3. Aviation Museum

You can see aircraft on the northern runway and taxiway from the Aviation Museum, although to photograph you'll need steps as there's too much in the way. Nevertheless, it is a good spot to note what's coming and going.

Airlines

Air China
Air Hong Kong
Air Macau
AirAsia
AirAsia X
All Nippon Airways
All Nippon Airways (Air Japan)
Asiana Airlines
Cargolux
Cathay Pacific
Cathay Pacific Cargo
Cebu Pacific
China Airlines
China Airlines Cargo
China Eastern Airlines
China Southern Airlines
Delta Air Lines
Dragonair
Emirates SkyCargo
EVA Air
EVA Air Cargo
FedEx Express
Garuda Indonesia
Hainan Airlines
Japan Airlines
Jetstar Asia Airways

KLM
Korean Air
Malaysia Airlines
Mandarin Airlines
MASkargo
Pacific East Asia Cargo Airlines
PacificFlier
Philippine Airlines
Shandong Airlines
Shanghai Airlines
Shenzhen Airlines
Sichuan Airlines
Singapore Airlines
Singapore Airlines Cargo
Spirit of Manila Airlines
Tiger Airways
Thai AirAsia
Thai Airways International
Trai Thien Air Cargo
TransAsia Airways
TransGlobal Airways
UNI Air
United Airlines
UPS Airlines
Vietnam Airlines
Xiamen Airlines

Hotels

Hotel Novotel Taipei Taoyuan Airport

1-1 Terminal South Road, Taoyuan County, Dayuan Township, 337 Taipei | +886 3398 0888
www.novotel.com

The closest hotel to the airport, and situated between the two runways alongside the roads which lead to the terminals. Higher rooms face either towards runway 05 or 06 thresholds, and as such you can get views of many (but not all) movements depending on the direction in use. The Aviation Museum is only a couple of minutes' walk from here.

Nearby Attractions

Aviation Museum

Taoyuan Airport | +886 3398 2677 | www.tycg.gov.tw

Situated between the runways and near the terminals, the Aviation Museum at Taoyuan Airport is a nice touch by the authorities for those interested in aircraft. It features a variety of displays, galleries, presentations and a number of preserved aircraft. These include a DC-3, HU-16 Albatross and a number of jet fighter aircraft. Open daily except Monday, 9am to 5pm. Adults NT$30, Children NT$20. A free shuttle bus runs between the terminal and museum.

Taipei Songshan Airport

(see separate entry)

Tianjin Binhai International Airport, China

TSN | ZBTJ

Tel: +86 22 2490 2012
Passengers: 4,637,299 (2008)

Overview

Tianjin is a large airport in north east China. In particular it is a large cargo centre, and also home to Okay Airways and Tianjin Airlines. The airport is also on the route networks of many Asian carriers.

The airport has undergone massive expansion and improvements over the past few years, opening a new state-of-the-art terminal in 2008 which is designed as part of a planned further modular expansion. This anticipated growth will see the number of movements at the airport increase steadily over coming years. A second parallel runway was also opened in 2009 to the east of the existing one, which again gives the airport more ability to expand.

Tianjin is also home to one of Airbus' final assembly lines, located at the south east corner of the airfield, which can yield some interesting aircraft. It is also home to a technical college and its collection of aircraft in the south west corner.

Spotting Locations

1. Technical College

Located at the south western corner of the airfield, south of the old terminal, is a technical college. It has a ramp of old airliners, including a Trident, Boeing 707, 727 and various other aircraft in various states parked outside. The road from the old terminal runs south and a side street runs past a football field and some basketball courts. Just past this is a view of the aircraft.

2. Inside Terminal

The new terminal has plenty of large windows overlooking the ramp. Photography is not acceptable, but you should be able to log of you are discrete. Unless on a domestic flight, you will have to pass through security and hold a boarding pass.

MAP

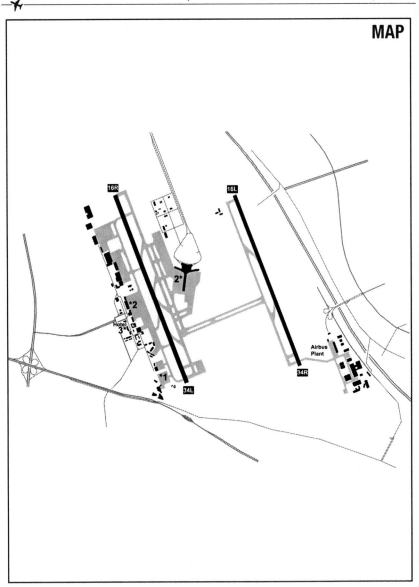

Frequencies

Tower	127.9
Tower	130.0
Ground	121.75
Approach	118.2
Approach	120.9
ATIS	126.4

Runways

16L/34R	10,499ft / 3,200m
16R/34L	11,811ft / 3,600m

3. Binhai International Hotel

The hotel, listed below, is possibly the best place to spot if you have any time to spend here. Rooms on higher floors facing the airport look over the old terminal, maintenance areas, old runway, cargo areas and across to the new terminal. The new runway is a bit distant, but aircraft can usually be read when they taxi closer.

Airlines

Air China

AirAsia X

Airstars

Asiana Airlines

China Eastern Airlines

China Southern Airlines

China West Air

Deer Jet

EVA Air

Grizodubova Air Company

Hainan Airlines

Hong Kong Airlines

Jade Cargo International

Japan Airlines

Juneyao Airlines

Korean Air

Lucky Air

Lufthansa Cargo

Okay Airways

Shandong Airlines

Shanghai Airlines

Shenzhen Airlines

Sichuan Airlines

Singapore Airlines Cargo

Tianjin Airlines

TransAVIAExport Airlines

Vladivostok Air

Volga-Dnepr

Xiamen Airlines

Hotels

Binhai International Airport Hotel

Binhai International Airport, Tianjin 300300

A modern hotel located near the original terminal at the airport, behind the Air China hangar. The hotel has high rooms facing the airport from which you will see all movements and can read off registrations. Photography can be tricky.

Nearby Attractions

Wuqing Air Base

A base for Chinese fighter aircraft around 20 miles north of the city. You can see aircraft movements from the roads around the airfield, but do not venture too close.

This page has been intentionally left blank.

Xiamen Gaoqi International Airport, China

XMN I ZSAM

Tel: +86 592 570 6078
Web: www.xiac.com.cn/en/
Passengers: 11,000,000 (2010)

Overview

Xiamen Gaoqi International is one of China's busiest both in terms of passengers and cargo traffic, although it is not a particularly big airport. Some expansion work is underway, but for now the terminal and runway are adequate for the airport's needs.

In terms of traffic, the airport mainly handles Chinese domestic traffic, with some international services to destinations in Asia and Europe.

Spotting Locations

1. Runway 05 Threshold

A small road in an industrial area on the north side of the airport overlooks the threshold of ruwnay 05. From here you can photograph aircraft approaching the runway, and also see across to the terminal gates.

2. Terminal

Inside the terminal, once through security, you have good views from all gates of aircraft parked there and at remote stands and the runway beyond.

Airlines

Air China	Dragonair
Air Macau	Hainan Airlines
All Nippon Airways	Juneyao Airlines
Chengdu Airlines	KLM
China Eastern Airlines	Korean Air
China Express Airlines	Malaysia Airlines
China Southern Airlines	Mandarin Airlines
China West Air	Northeast Airlines

MAP

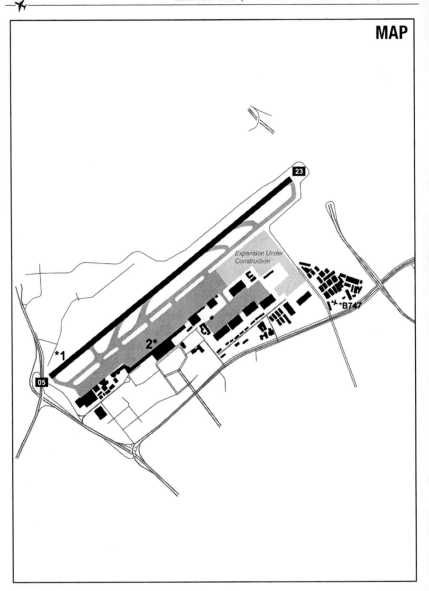

Frequencies

Tower	118.25
Tower	130.0
Ground	121.7
Approach	119.05
Approach	121.35
ATIS	126.25

Runways

5/23   11,155ft / 3,400m

Philippine Airlines

Shandong Airlines

Shanghai Airlines

Shenzhen Airlines

Sichuan Airlines

SilkAir

Spring Airlines

Thai Airways International

TransAsia Airways

UNI Air

Xiamen Airlines

Hotels

Xiamen International Garden Hotel

50 Xiangun 1st Road, Gaoqi International Airport Xiamen, Fujian Province | (718) 446-4800
www.marriott.com

Located just outside the airport hotel, this is the ideal place to stay. It is a standard airport hotel, but has clean rooms and plenty of amenities. It has a free shuttle to/from the airport. Some higher rooms have distant views of aircraft movements.

Nearby Attractions

University Boeing 747

This former British Airways Boeing 747-236 G-BDXB is parked in a corner of the airport and used as a training aid by the local university. It is marked on the map, and possible to see it from the surrounding roads.

This page has been intentionally left blank.

Xi'an Xianyang International Airport, China

XIYI ZLXY

Tel: +86
Web: www.xxia.com.cn
Passengers: 15,294,948 (2009)

Overview

Xi'an Xianyang is a large airport which has been growing steadily over recent years. It is located in the north west of China. It handles a large list of airlines, both carry passengers and cargo, and is one of the top ten busiest airports in the country. It is a hub airport for China Eastern Airlines.

At the time of writing, Xianyang is undergoing an expansion which will see an additional runway being built parallel to the existing one, and a third terminal. Combined, these expansions will raise the annual passenger limit to 26 million and allow the airport to grow.

Spotting Locations

1. Terminal Windows

The windows in the departure lounges of Terminal 1 and 2 are tall and clean, offering plenty of views of the apron and runway beyond.

2. Dornier Ramp

There is a ramp south west of the terminal which is home to a number of Dornier 328 aircraft, and most will be present on the average visit. It is possible to log these, but quite difficult to find. Using a taxi or your own car is these best way to quickly reach and log aircraft here.

Airlines

Air China
Asiana Airlines
Beijing Capital Airlines
China Airlines
China Eastern Airlines

MAP

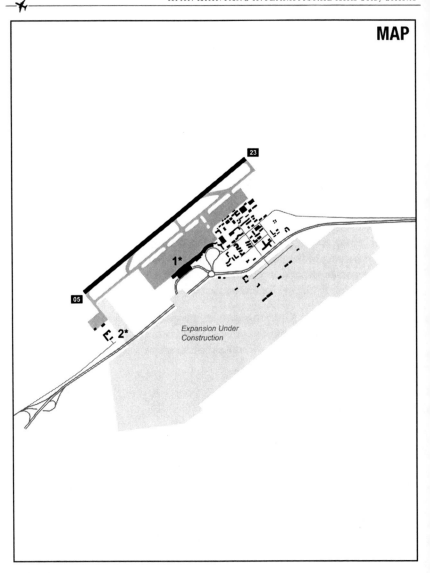

23

1*

05

2*

Expansion Under Construction

Frequencies

Tower	118.15
Tower	124.3
Ground	121.8
Ground	124.3
Approach	119.6
Approach	126.55
ATIS	127.45

Runways

5/23   9,842ft / 3,000m

China Southern Airlines
Hainan Airlines
Joy Air
Juneyao Airlines
Korean Air
Shandong Airlines
Shanghai Airlines
Sichuan Airlines
Spring Airlines
Xiamen Airlines

Hotels

Shanxi Aviation Hotel

Xianyang Airport, Xi'an, China 712035 | +86 29 8879 7000

Three star hotel a short walk from the terminal, with all the modern amenities you need. Can often be fully booked. Rooms on 8th or 9th floors facing the airport have views of aircraft on the ground and using the runway. If you have a SBS, you will be able to tie up distant movements and those at night.

Nearby Attractions

Xi'an is surrounded by military airfields. Each has its own based fleet of aircraft and security is naturally very tight. Streets around these airfield may offer fleeting glimpses of aircraft as they land or depart. Airfields include Huxian (22 miles south of Xianyang), Guowangcun (22 miles east), and Yanliang (32 miles north east).

Terracotta Army

No visit to the Xi'an region is complete without a trip to see the famous Terracotta Army. It is located to the east of the city, at Lintong. Dating from 210BC, there are thousands of figures that have been unearthed. You can visit the Museum of the Qin Terracotta Warriors and Horses along with the neighbouring Qin Shi Huang Mausoleum on one ticket.

This page has been intentionally left blank.

Airports in Indonesia

1. Denpasar Bali Airport
2. Jakarta Soekarno-Hatta Airport

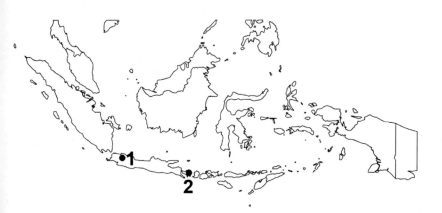

This page has been intentionally left blank.

Denpasar Bali, Indonesia

DPS | WADD

Web: www.ngurahrai-airport.co.id

Passengers: 9,625,433 (2009)

Overview

Denpasar Ngurah Rai International is the third busiest airport in Indonesia, and a very important holiday destination within Asia - particularly amongst Australians. The airport sees a good mix of exotic domestic aircraft and large international carriers on a daily basis. Unfortunately due to terrorist activity the airport has become much more secure and increasingly more difficult to spot at; the best spotting location has now disappointingly been fenced off.

Spotting Locations

1. Kutra Beach

This was once an amazing position for photographing aircraft on the runway and taxiways close up. However, recently fences have been erected on the breakwater which prevents you getting close and blocks any decent photography. Nevertheless, you can still see aircraft movements from this beach and read registrations.

2. Jimbaran

On the south side of the airport, the village of Jimbaran has a number of streets which lead to crash gates fronting the runway. It is easy to photograph aircraft through holes in the fence here, however security will often move spotters on from these locations. Jimbaran's beach also has opportunities to watch movements, but is no good for photography.

3. Terminal

On the departures level of the terminal, a narrow corridor can be found which has large windows overlooking the apron and runway. Photography is not ideal due to the glass, but it is the only worthwhile spot inside the building.

MAP

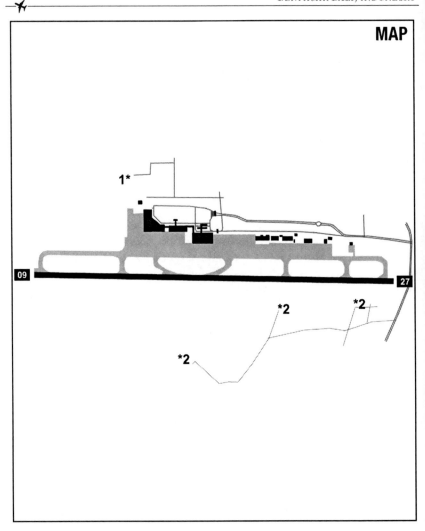

Frequencies

Frequencies	
Tower	118.1
Tower	118.5
Ground	118.9
Director	119.3
Director	119.7
ATIS	126.2

Runways

9/27   9,842ft / 3,000m

Airlines

Aeroflot
AirAsia
Batavia Air
Cathay Pacific
China Airlines
China Eastern Airlines
EVA Air
Garuda Indonesia
Garuda (Citilink)
Hong Kong Airlines
Indonesia AirAsia
Indonesia Air Transport
Jetstar Airways
KLM
Korean Air
Lion Air
Malaysian Airlines

Mandala Airlines
Merpati Nusantara Airlines
Pacific Blue
Qatar Airways
Shanghai Airlines
Shenzhen Airlines
Singapore Airlines
Skywest
Sriwijaya Air
Strategic Airlines
Thai AirAsia
Thai Airways International
Transaero
TransNusa
Trigana Air
UNI Air
Wings Air

Hotels

There are no hotels with views of Denpasar Bali Airport. However, as a resort there are plenty of hotels within a short driving distance. Some may have distant views of aircraft on approach.

Nearby Attractions

N/A

This page has been intentionally left blank.

Jakarta Soekarno-Hatta, Indonesia

CGK | WIII

Web: www.jakartasoekarnohattaairport.com
Passengers: 32,466,823 (2009)

Overview

Jakarta Soekarno-Hatta Airport is somewhere all enthusiasts should visit whenever possible as it has become a place where ageing airliners from the West congregate in storage and maintenance. It is also a place where these airliners live on with the many domestic airlines in Indonesia.

The airport is the busiest in the country and has three terminals, with the two main ones having viewing galleries. The famous hotel in the International Terminal is also an excellent place to stay and spot in comfort. You can travel freely between the three terminals using the transfer bus.

Spotting Locations

1. Domestic Terminal

The Domestic Terminal has a number of so-called waving galleries along its length. Each is free to enter and offers a slightly different view to others. It is best to start at one end and work your way along. They offer good opportunities to photograph domestic aircraft, and some galleries look over the maintenance and storage areas. It is difficult to see anything at the International Terminal from here.

2. International Terminal

The International Terminal has a viewing gallery on the western end of the building. From here you'll see most of the movements on the northern runway and traffic using this terminal. It is difficult to see anything at the Domestic Terminal from here.

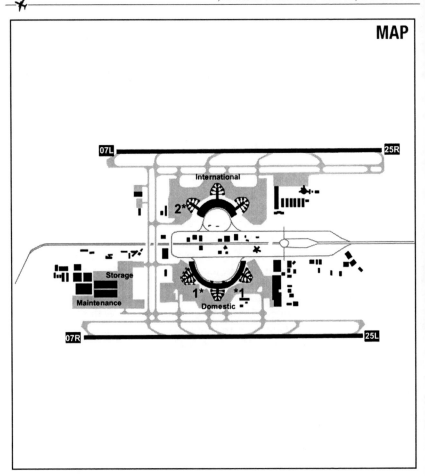

MAP

Frequencies

Tower	118.2
Tower	118.75
Ground	121.6
Ground	121.75
Jakarta Info	129.7
Pabelokan Info	129.8
Clearance Delivery	121.95
Arrivals	125.45
Arrivals	135.9
Approach	119.75
Approach	127.9
Approach	127.95
ATIS	126.85

Runways

7L/25R	11,811ft / 3,600m
7R/25L	12,007ft / 3,660m

Airlines

AirAsia
Air China
Airfast Indonesia
All Nippon Airways
Batavia Air
Cardig Air
Cargo Garuda Indonesia
Cathay Pacific
Cathay Pacific Cargo
Cebu Pacific
China Airlines
China Airlines Cargo
China Southern Airlines
Emirates
Etihad Airways
EVA Air
EVA Air Cargo
Express Air
FedEx Express

Garuda Indonesia
Garuda (Citilink)
Indonesia AirAsia
Japan Airlines
Jetstar Airways
Kartika Airlines
KLM
KLM Cargo
Korean Air
Korean Air Cargo
Kuwait Airways
Lion Air
Lion Air (Wings Air)
Lufthansa
Malaysia Airlines
MASkargo
Merpati Nusantara
Airlines
Mihin Lanka

Philippine Airlines
Qatar Airways
Qantas
Republic Express Airlines
Royal Brunei Airlines
Saudi Arabian Airlines
Shenzhen Airlines
Singapore Airlines
Sriwijaya Air
Thai AirAsia
Thai Airways International
Tiger Airways
Transmile Air Services
Tri-MG Intra Asia Airlines
Turkish Airlines
Valuair
Yemenia

Hotels

Jakarta Airport Hotel

Terminal 2E, Soekarno-Hatta International Airport, Jakarta 19110 | +62 21 559 0008
www.jakartaairporthotel.com

The only place to spend the night watching the action at Jakarta Soekarno-Hatta if you
can arrange a room. This airport is situated upstairs in the International Terminal and
all rooms look out over the gates and northern runway. The corridor leading to the rooms
has windows looking towards the domestic side of the airport and maintenance areas.
Perfectly nice place to stay, but can be expensive and is often fully booked.

Sheraton Bandara Hotel

Bandara Soekarno-Hatta International Airport, Jakarta 19110 | +62 21 559 7777
www.starwoodhotels.com

A very nice hotel located just outside the airport entrance. Its orientation is towards
the southern (domestic) part of the airport and many rooms have views of aircraft
approaching runway 25L. The hotel is associated with the neighbouring golf course and
can be quite expensive.

Nearby Attractions

Jakarta Halim Perdanakusuma Airport

Formerly the city's main airport until CGK opened in 1985, Halim still handles some cargo, domestic and military transport flights. Like CGK, it is also home to many stored older airliners on its south side. It is also home to air taxi and domestic operator Deraya. Although not as easy as it used to be, recent reports state it is still possible to get airside photography access at Halim. Otherwise, there are few spotting locations from outside the airport. Halim is located within the city; around 20 minutes drive from CGK.

Airports in Japan

1. Fukuoka Airport
2. Nagoya Chubu Centrair International Airport
3. Osaka Itami International Airport
4. Osaka Kansai International Airport
5. Sapporo New Chitose Airport
6. Tokyo Haneda International Airport
7. Tokyo Narita International Airport

This page has been intentionally left blank.

Fukuoka Airport, Japan

FUK | RJFF

Tel: +81 92 473 2518
Web: www.fuk-ab.co.jp/english/
Passengers: 18,100,000 (2006)

Overview

Fukuoka Airport handles a mix of domestic and intra-Asian flights from a variety of airlines. It is the fourth busiest airport in Japan and is bursting at the seams due to its enclosed location near the centre of the city. There are three domestic passenger terminals - 1, 2 and 3 - on the northern side of the single runway, and an International Terminal on the opposite side. A smaller cargo terminal is situated alongside the International Terminal.

As with most Japanese airports, enthusiasts are catered for by observation decks on all terminals.

Spotting Locations

1. Domestic Terminal 1 Observation Deck

All three domestic terminals have their own observation deck. The one at Terminal 1 is outdoor and accessed from floor 2F in the departures area. It is free of charge and open from 7am to 8pm. This is a good all-round location for aircraft using the runway and domestic terminals. Large fences front the deck, which can hinder photography but is usually acceptable.

2. Domestic Terminal 1 Observation Room

Accessed via a spiral staircase from floor 3F, Terminal 1's alternative observation area is indoors and fronted by glass windows. This can sometimes hinder photography, but the views are great and it's a nice warm place to spot in harsh weather. Free of charge, and open 7am to 8pm.

3. Domestic Terminal 2 Observation Deck

You can access this rooftop deck from floor 3F near the games room. It is a slightly more spacious area to spot from, which has glass windows instead of fences. The glass is usually clean enough to take photographs through. Views are of the southern end of the domestic terminal and the runway. You can see across to the International Terminal too. Free of charge, and open from 7am to 9.30pm.

MAP

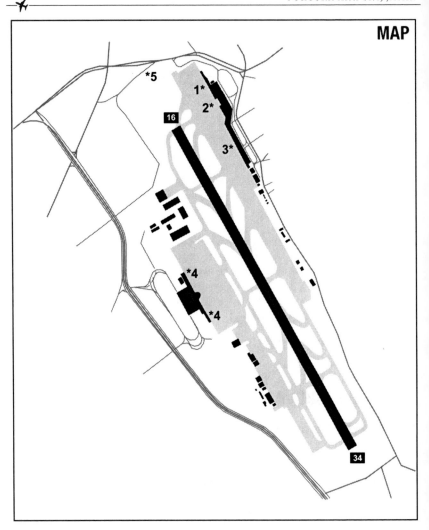

Frequencies

Tower	118.4
Tower	126.2
Ground	121.7
Clearance Delivery	121.925
Approach	119.1
Approach	120.7
Approach	121.125
Departure	119.7
Terminal Control Area	121.275
ATIS	127.2

Runways

16/34   9,186ft / 2,800m

4. International Terminal Observation Decks

There are two observation decks atop the International Terminal and accessed from either end of the building. These have views over the international gates, runway, and across to the domestic terminals. The decks are surrounded by glass, so photographs are not always perfect. Free of charge and open from 7.30am to 8.30pm.

5. Runway 16

There are a few points around the perimeter fence close to the end of Runway 16. From these you can take good unobstructed views of aircraft landing on this runway, and you'll often find other spotters here. You can see some movements on the ground through the fence. You can reach these points by walking alongside the fence from Terminal 2 for around 15 minutes.

Airlines

Air Busan
Air China
Amakusa Airlines
All Nippon Airways
ANA (Air Next)
ANA (Air Nippon)
Asiana Airlines
Cathay Pacific
China Airlines
China Eastern Airlines
China Southern Airlines
Continental Airlines
Dragonair
EVA Air
Fuji Dream Airlines
Japan Airlines
Japan Airlines (J-Air)
Japan Airlines (Japan Air Commuter)
Japan Airlines (Japan Transocean Air)
Korean Air
Philippine Airlines
Skymark Airlines
Singapore Airlines
Thai Airways International
Vietnam Airlines

Hotels

There are no hotels at Fukuoka Airport. The nearest recommended hotel is:

The B Hakata

1-3-9 Hakataekimae-minami Hakata, 812-0016 | +81 92 415 3333
www.ishinhotels.com/theb-hakata/en/

Only ten minutes' drive from the International Terminal, this modern, clean hotel is a good choice. Located in Hakata. All rooms have good amenities, and rates are reasonable.

Nearby Attractions

N/A

Nagoya Chubu Centrair International Airport, Japan

NGO | RJGG

Tel: +81 569 38 1195
Web: www.centrair.jp
Passengers: 10,800,000 (2009)

Overview

Chubu Centrair International is another of Japan's man-made island airports, built offshore around 22 miles south of the city of Nagoya. It is currently the country's 8th busiest and handles a good mix of Japanese, Asian and carriers from further afield.

The airport has a single runway, although it plans to construct a second, parallel runway in the future to cope with planned growth. There is one large terminal, with domestic flights using the southern and, and international flights using the northern end. The cargo terminal is to the north.

Spotting Locations

1. Observation Deck

By far the easiest and best location for spotting at Chubu, the official Observation Deck runs along the top of the central pier atop the terminal. This is a large, popular deck which is open from 7am-9pm, free of charge. It has tall wire fencing running along its length, but it is still possible to poke a camera through to take photographs.

2. Domestic Terminal Gate Area

If the weather isn't good enough to be outside, you can shelter in the domestic gate area of the terminal where large windows offer plenty of views of the aircraft and runway beyond. You can't see the international gates from here, but aircraft will be visible when using the runway.

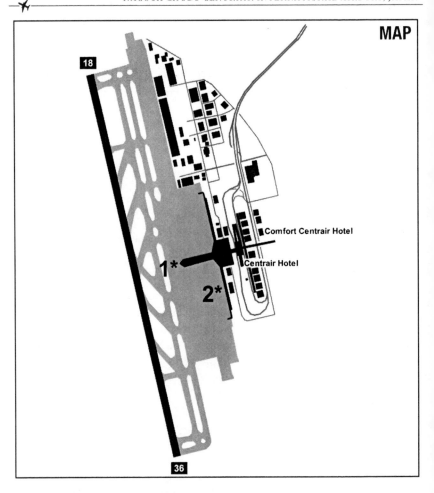

Frequencies

Tower	118.85
Tower	126.2
Ground	121.8
Ground	126.2
Clearance Delivery	121.85
Clearance Delivery	126.2
Approach	119.175
Approach	121.05
Departure	120.0
Radar	125.5
Terminal Control Area	119.25
Terminal Control Area	121.175
ATIS	121.075

Runways

18/36   11,483ft / 3,500m

Airlines

Air China	Finnair
Air Hong Kong	Garuda Indonesia
AirBridgeCargo Airlines	Japan Airlines
All Nippon Airways	Japan Airlines (JAL Express)
ANA (Air Central)	Japan Airlines (JALways)
Asiana Airlines	Japan Airlines (Japan Transocean Air)
Asiana Cargo	Jeju Air
Cathay Pacific	Kalitta Air
China Airlines	Korean Air
China Eastern Airlines	Korean Air Cargo
China Southern Airlines	Lufthansa
Continental Micronesia	Nippon Cargo Airlines
Delta Air Lines	Philippine Airlines
DHL Express	Singapore Airlines
Etihad Airways	Thai Airways International
EVA Air	UPS Airlines
Evergreen International	Vietnam Airlines

Hotels

Centrair Hotel

1-1 Centrair, Tokoname | +81 569 38 1111 | www.centrairhotel.jp

The closest hotel to the airport terminal. It is tall, and upper rooms facing the airport have views of movements on the runway and domestic side of the terminal.

Comfort Hotel Centrair International

4-2-3 Centrair, Tokoname | +81 569 38 7211 | www.comfortinn.com

A more affordable option than the Centrair Hotel, and still linked to the terminal via a covered walkway. This hotel, however, has few, if any, views of movements. Nevertheless, it is only a short walk to the excellent Observation Deck.

Nearby Attractions

Nagoya Komaki Airport

The former international airport before Chubu took over in 2006; Komaki is still an active airport with passenger flights through Fuji Dream Airlines and J-Air on behalf of Japan Airlines. Additionally, the airport is a busy JASDF base with many transport types passing through. Viewing is possible from a nice observation deck atop the passenger terminal. The airport is situated in the north of the city.

This page has been intentionally left blank.

Osaka Itami Airport, Japan

ITM | RJOO

Tel: +81 6 6856 6781
Web: osaka-airport.co.jp/en/
Passengers: 18,948,300 (2005)

Overview

The original airport for Osaka, Itami is now relegated to domestic operations as Kansai International expands on its man-made island to the south of the city. Itami is surrounded on all sides by the city and, despite its relegation to being the city's second airport, it is still the third busiest in Japan. Here you will primarily see the country's two main operators - Japan Airlines and All Nippon Airways (and their feeder carriers) operating throughout the country with various aircraft types.

Spotting Locations

1. Observation Deck

The airport's observation deck is located on top of the terminal building and overlooks the runways and many of the gates. Photography is good from here, although air bridges can get in the way of closer shots. The observation deck is open from 8am-10pm and is free of charge. You can access it on the 3rd floor.

2. Itami Sky Park

Situated on the opposite side of the airport, the Sky Park is another viewing area provided for spotters. This garden-like structure has various levels allowing photography above the fence of aircraft on the main 14R/32L runway. The Sky Park extends for quite a distance along the airport perimeter. It is an excellent spot in good weather, and free to use.

3. Runway 32L

A track runs by the end of runway 32L which is a good place to photograph aircraft just before touchdown and whilst on the runway. It is possible to drive along the track, which links two city roads. Be careful not to cause an obstruction.

MAP

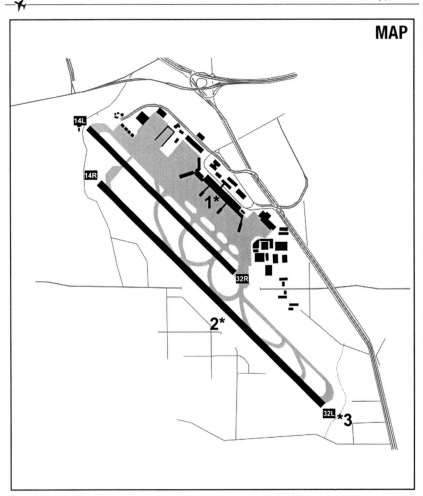

Frequencies

Tower	118.1
Tower	126.2
Ground	121.7
Terminal Control	121.1
Ground Control	125.1
Ground Control	127.5
Ground Control	134.1
Clearance Delivery	118.8
Departure	119.5
Departure	125.3
Approach	120.45
ATIS	128.6

Runways

14L/32R 5,997ft / 1,828m
14R/32L 9,843ft / 3,000m

Airlines

All Nippon Airways
ANA (Air Nippon)
ANA (Air Nippon Network)
ANA (Ibex Airlines)
Ibex Airlines
Japan Airlines
Japan Airlines (J-Air)
Japan Airlines (JAL Express)
Japan Airlines (Japan Air Commuter)

Hotels

Hotel Itami

+81 72 784 2600 | www.hotel-itami.net

A modern hotel on the western side of the airport, only a short walk from the Itami Sky Park viewing area alongside the runway. There are no views of movements from the hotel, however.

Nearby Attractions

Kobe Airport

A small, mainly domestic airport built on an island off the city of Kobe. It is around 30 miles by road from Itami Airport. Kobe handles flights by ANA and Skymark Airlines, and has an excellent observation deck atop the terminal.

Osaka Kansai International

(see separate entry)

This page has been intentionally left blank.

Osaka Kansai Airport, Japan

KIX | RJBB

Tel: +81 724 55 2093
Web: www.kiac.co.jp/en/
Passengers: 13,516,000 (2009)

Overview

Osaka is Japan's second largest city and Kansai Airport is its new main airport, having replaced Itami (see separate entry) when it opened in 1994. Itami remains open as a domestic airport, however Kansai is now the larger and busier gateway. It was constructed on a man-made island in Osaka Bay and has already expanded with a second runway. A large area has also been set aside for an additional terminal, and it is anticipated that a third runway will also be built. All major Japanese and Asian airlines fly to Kansai, and a dedicated Observation Hall is the only place you need to spot from.

Spotting Locations

1. Observation Hall

The official spotting location at Kansai is an elevated platform at the eastern end of the airport, close to the threshold of runway 24L. It has excellent views over this runway and the terminal gates, so you won't miss any aircraft or registrations. Photography is also good, with the classic view of aircraft passing over the road bridge possible. The Observation Hall is free and open 9am-9pm (10pm at weekends).

Airlines

Air Busan
Air China
Air China Cargo
Air France
Air Hong Kong
Air India
Air Macau
Air New Zealand

Air Nippon
Aircalin
Aircompany Yakutia
Alitalia
All Nippon Airways
ANA Cargo
Asiana Airlines
Asiana Cargo

MAP

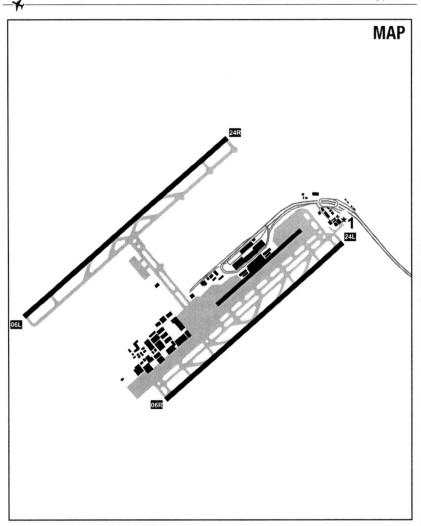

Frequencies

Tower	118.2
Tower	126.2
Ground	121.6
Terminal Control	121.1
Clearance Delivery	121.9
Clearance Delivery	126.2
Departure	119.2
Approach	120.25
Approach	125.5
ATIS	127.85

Runways

6R/24L	11,483ft / 3,500m
6L/24R	13,123ft / 4,000m

Cathay Pacific
Cathay Pacific Cargo
Cebu Pacific
China Airlines
China Airlines Cargo
China Cargo Airlines
China Eastern Airlines
China Postal Airlines
China Southern Airlines
Continental Micronesia
Delta Air Lines
Dragonair
EgyptAir
Emirates
EVA Air
EVA Air Cargo
FedEx Express
Finnair
Garuda Indonesia
Hainan Airlines
Hong Kong Express Airways
Japan Airlines
Japan Airlines (J-Air)
Japan Airlines (JALways)
Japan Airlines (JAL Express)
Japan Airlines (Japan Transocean Air)
Jeju Air

Jetstar Airways
Jetstar Asia Airways
KLM
Korean Air
Korean Air Cargo
Lufthansa
Lufthansa Cargo
Malaysia Airlines
MIAT Mongolian Airlines
Nippon Cargo Airlines
Philippine Airlines
Polar Air Cargo
Qatar Airways
Shandong Airlines
Shanghai Airlines Cargo
Shenzhen Airlines
Singapore Airlines
Singapore Airlines Cargo
StarFlyer
Thai Airways International
Turkish Airlines
United Airlines
UPS Airlines
Uzbekistan Airways
Vietnam Airlines
Xiamen Airlines

Hotels

Hotel Nikko Kansai Airport

1 Senshu-kuko Kita, Izumisano-shi, Osaka 549-0001 | +81 72 455 1111 | www.nikkokix.com

A large hotel situated just outside the terminal complex and only a short walk from the observation hall. The hotel doesn't really have any views of movements.

Kansai Airport Washington Hotel

1-7 Rinku Orai-kita, Izumisano-shi, Osaka 598-8522 | +81 72 461 2222 | www.wh-rsv.com

An alternative to the Nikko, the Washington Hotel is located just across the bridge on the mainland. It is a tall hotel, and upper rooms facing the airport have (distant) views of aircraft arriving and departing. Use of a SBS will help you tie up movements.

Nearby Attractions

Osaka Itami Airport

(see separate entry)

Kobe Airport

A small, mainly domestic airport built on an island off the city of Kobe. It is around 25 miles by road from Osaka city centre. Kobe handles flights by ANA and Skymark Airlines, and has an excellent observation deck atop the terminal.

Sapporo New Chitose Airport, Japan

CTS | RJCC

Tel: +81 123 23 0111
Web: www.new-chitose-airport.jp/en/
Passengers: 18,082,925 (2009)

Overview

New Chitose Airport is a joint venture with Chitose JASDF Air Base. The two entities are linked via taxiways, but do not usually share runways or other facilities. Originally both airports shared the same runways, but the 'new' came into effect when the 01/19 runways and semi-circular domestic terminal were built. International flights are handled from a new terminal built on the air base side in 2010. New Chitose Airport suffers operating restrictions by the government due to the adjacent base. As such, international flights only permitted on Tuesdays and Wednesdays from 12-4pm, and all day Saturday and Sunday. Regardless, New Chitose is still the busiest Japanese airport after Narita and Haneda.

The JASDF base handles all of the presidential Boeing 747 aircraft, and many other military and transport types. However, due to the sensitive nature of the operations, it is not advised to loiter around the base.

Spotting Locations

1. Observation Deck

The observation deck is on top of the circular domestic terminal. It is accessed from the restaurant area on the third floor, and opens from 9am-5pm daily (although closed in winter). It is a good spot for photography and all movements will be seen. Entry free.

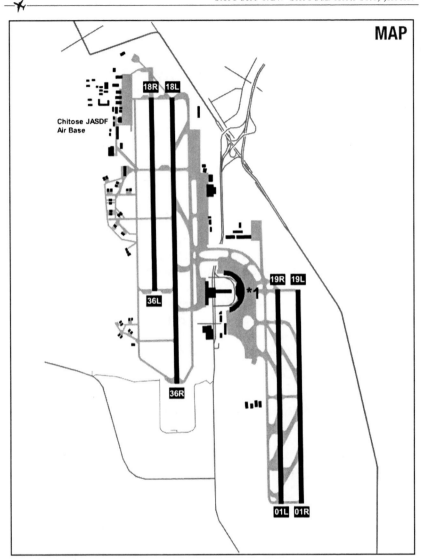

MAP

Frequencies

Tower	118.8
Tower	126.2
Ground	121.6
Departure	124.7
Approach	120.1
Clearance Delivery	121.9
Terminal Control	127.7
ATIS	128.6

Runways

1L/19R	9,843ft / 3,000m
1R/19L	9,843ft / 3,000m
18L/36R	9,843ft / 3,000m
18R/36L	8,858ft / 2,700m

Airlines

Air China	EVA Air
Air Do	Hong Kong Express Airways
All Nippon Airways	Japan Airlines
Cathay Pacific	Japan Airlines (Hokkaido Air System)
China Airlines	Japan Airlines (Japan Air Commuter)
China Eastern Airlines	Korean Air
China Southern Airlines	Sakhalin Airlines
Continental Micronesia	Skymark Airlines
Eastar Jet	UNI Air

Hotels

Mitsui Urban Hotel

New Chitose Airport Terminal Building, Chitose, Hokkaido 066-0012

This affordable hotel is located in the domestic terminal and thus ideal for the spotter. Rooms facing the action are perfect for watching movements, although not very good for photography due to the glass.

Nearby Attractions

Sapporo Okadama Airport

A small commuter airport close to downtown Sapporo. It is served by Hokkaido Air System who link it with other airports on the island with turboprops. JASDF also use the airport, and there is a busy general aviation scene. You can view from the terminal, or from a play area close to the end of runway 14.

This page has been intentionally left blank.

Tokyo Haneda Airport, Japan

HND | RJTT

Tel: +81 364 28 0888
Web: www.tokyo-airport-bldg.co.jp/en/
Passengers: 62,100,754 (2009)

Overview

Haneda is one of the best airports to spot at in Japan. It has provided observation decks on all terminals, including the newly-opened International Terminal, giving you plenty of space to observe the vast number of aircraft passing through the airport.

Although Haneda is no longer the official main airport for Tokyo (Narita holds this position), it has undergone a number of expansions and improvements, including the new terminal and a fourth runway opened in 2010. Many more international flights have now also been approved and, combined with the large number of domestic and intra-Asian flights; it makes it a very busy airport indeed.

Spotting Locations

1. Terminal 1 Observation Deck

Terminal 1's observation deck overlooks that terminal and the new International Terminal across runway 16R/34L. It is free to enter, and open from 6.30am to 10pm daily. The deck is accessed from the centre of the building via lift or escalator. Although there are tall fences around the deck, there are enlarged holes for sticking camera lenses through. Photography is best in the morning.

2. Terminal 2 Observation Deck

On the opposite side to the Terminal 1 deck, this one overlooks runway 16L/34R. It is also open from 6.30am to 10pm daily, and free of charge. This deck is better for photography from mid-morning onwards.

3. International Terminal Observation Deck

This new terminal also has a free deck on top, which is open the same times and free of charge. It looks over the international gates, runway 16R/34L and across to Terminal 1. Light is best from mid-morning, but again you'll have to grapple with the high fence and limited holes to stick a lens through.

MAP

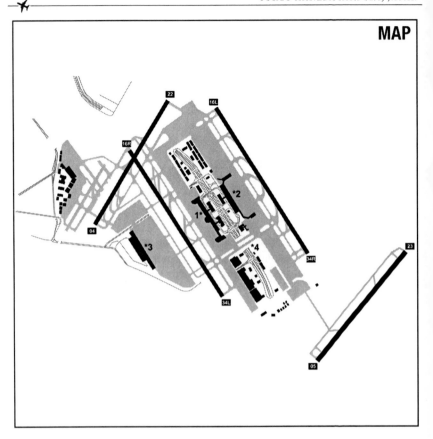

Frequencies

Tower	118.1
Tower	118.8
Tower	124.35
Tower	126.2
Ground	118.225
Ground	121.7
Clearance Delivery	121.825
Clearance Delivery	121.875
Departure	120.8
Departure	126.0
Departure	127.6
Approach	119.1
Approach	119.7
Approach	126.5
Terminal Control Area	124.75
ATIS	128.8

Runways

16R/34L	9,843ft / 3,000m
16L/34R	9,843ft / 3,000m
4/22	8,202ft / 2,500m
5/23	8,202ft / 2,500m

4. Taxiway Fence

A short walk south of Terminal 1 and 2, passing underneath the taxiway, you will be able to get a spot alongside the taxiway which is close to aircraft as they pass. The fence can be a problem to get good photographs, however. To reach the spot you'll have to double back on yourself after passing through the tunnel in order to get up to the fence.

Airlines

Air Canada
Air China
AirAsia X
American Airlines
All Nippon Airways
ANA (Air Japan)
ANA (Air Nippon)
ANA (Air Nippon Network)
Asiana Airlines
British Airways
Cathay Pacific
China Airlines
China Eastern Airlines
Delta Air Lines
EVA Air
Hawaiian Airlines
Hokkaido International Airlines
Japan Airlines
Japan Airlines (J-Air)
Japan Airlines (JAL Express)
Japan Airlines (Japan Transocean Air)
Korean Air
MIAT Mongolian Airlines
Malaysia Airlines
Shanghai Airlines
Singapore Airlines
Skymark Airlines
Skynet Asia Airways
StarFlyer
Thai Airways International

Hotels

Haneda Excel Hotel Tokyo

3-4-2 Haneda-airport Ota, 144-0041 Tokyo | +81 3 5756 6000 | www.tokyuhotelsjapan.com/en/

Linked to Terminal 2, this hotel offers the best views at the airport. Ask for a higher floor room facing the airport. It is quite expensive to stay at this hotel, but the location is superb.

Nearby Attractions

Tokyo Narita Airport

(see separate entry)

Tokyo Narita Airport, Japan

NRT | RJAA
Tel: +81 476 34 8000
Web: www.narita-airport.jp/en/
Passengers: 29,186,494 (2009)

Overview

Narita is Tokyo's primary airport, although it shares the city's air traffic with Haneda. Narita is further from the city, and has faced numerous problems in legal wrangles with land owners, meaning one runway was never used and another restricted to half its planned length.

Narita has two passenger terminals and a large cargo terminal. Japan Airlines handle maintenance of their fleet here, also. Most of the world's major carriers, both passenger and cargo, fly to Narita making it a truly international hub and the gateway to Japan. It is linked to the city via dedicated rail stations under each terminal.

Spotting Locations

1. Terminal 1 Observation Deck

The largest of the official spotting locations at Narita. It is located atop Terminal 1 and is free to enter. It has views over the gates, taxiways and the main runway, and photography is good but through a fence. It is accessed from level 4F inside the terminal, and open from 7am to 9pm.

2. Terminal 2 Observation Decks

Terminal 2 has two observation decks - one either side of the pier. They are both free to enter, and open from 7am to 9pm. The southern deck has better views of the taxiways, but the northern one has views of some gates that are not visible to the other. Photography is possible through enlarged holes in the fence, and light is best in the afternoon.

3. Aviation Museum

Whilst the Aviation Museum is worth a visit in its own right, it also features an observation deck which is good for views of aircraft approaching runway 34L

MAP

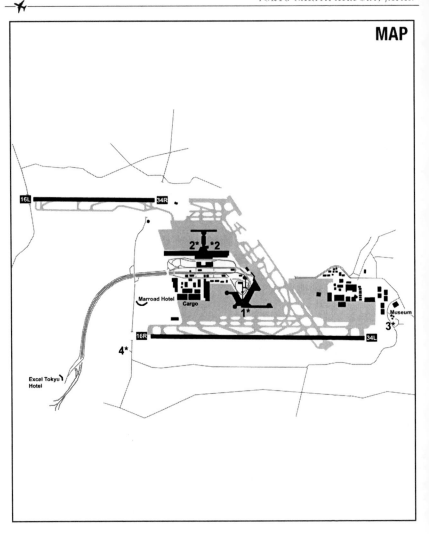

Frequencies

Tower	118.2
Tower	118.35
Ground	121.95
Ramp Control	121.6
Clearance Delivery	121.9
Departure	119.6
Departure	124.2
Approach	124.4
Terminal Control Area	119.45
ATIS	128.25

Runways

16R/34L   13,123ft / 4,000m
16L/34R   8,202ft / 2,500m

and on the taxiways linking it. It makes for good photographs. If you don't have a car, take bus from Terminal 1 South Wing stop No. 30.

4. Sakura no Yama Park

Situated near the end of runway 16R and ideal if aircraft are landing on this runway. Good for photographs, although the perimeter fence can sometimes get in the way. You also have good views over the western side of the airport. Many people come here, although you'll need a car to get there. It is a 15 minute walk from the Marroad Hotel.

Airlines

Aeroflot	Continental Airlines	Pakistan International
Aeroflot-Cargo	Continental Micronesia	Philippine Airlines
Aeromexico	Delta Air Lines	Polar Air Cargo
Air Canada	Edelweiss Air	Qantas
Air China	EgyptAir	Qatar Airways
Air France	Emirates	Scandinavian Airlines
Air France Cargo	Etihad Airways	Shenzhen Airlines
Air Hong Kong	EVA Air	Singapore Airlines
Air India	FedEx Express	Singapore Airlines Cargo
Air Macau	Finnair	SriLankan Airlines
Air New Zealand	Garuda Indonesia	Swiss International
Air Tahiti Nui	Hong Kong Airlines	Air Lines
AirBridgeCargo Airlines	Iran Air	Thai Airways International
Aircalin	Japan Airlines	Transaero Airlines
Alitalia	Japan Airlines	Turkish Airlines
All Nippon Airways	(JAL Express)	United Airlines
American Airlines	Japan Airlines (JALways)	UPS Airlines
ANA (Air Central)	Japan Airlines (Japan	Uzbekistan Airways
ANA (Air Japan)	Transocean Air)	Vietnam Airlines
ANA (Air Nippon)	Jetstar Airways	Virgin Atlantic
ANA (Ibex Airlines)	KLM	Vladivostok Air
Asiana Airlines	KLM Cargo	
Atlas Air	Korean Air	
Austrian Airlines	Korean Air Cargo	
British Airways	Lufthansa	
Cathay Pacific	Lufthansa Cargo	
Cathay Pacific Cargo	Malaysia Airlines	
China Airlines	MASkargo	
China Cargo Airlines	MIAT Mongolian Airlines	
China Eastern Airlines	Narita Heli Express	
China Southern Airlines	Nippon Cargo Airlines	

Hotels

Marroad International Hotel

763-1 Komaino, Narita-shi, Chiba 286-0121 | +81 476 30 2222
www.toto-motors.co.uk/marroad/narita/

Situated close to the threshold of runway 16R. If you ask for a room facing the airport, you will have views of this runway, the cargo apron and part of Terminal 1. Photographs are possible and most movements can be logged. The hotel's top-floor restaurant also has good views. Reasonably priced.

Narita Excel Tokyu Hotel

31 Oyama, Narita-shi, Chiba 286-0131 | +81 476 33 0133 | www.tokyuhotelsjapan.com/en/

Again, situated close to runway 16R and airport facing rooms have views of most movements. Photography is not good from here, however. A little more expensive than the Marroad, but worth it for seeing more movements and the arrivals screens in the lobby.

Nearby Attractions

Museum of Aeronautical Sciences

Located close to the end of runway 34L and with its own observation deck, the Aviation Museum has a nice little collection of civil aircraft and helicopters. The largest preserved type is a NAMC YS-11 airliner. The museum is open 10am-5pm Tuesday-Sunday (daily in January, May and August), with a 500 yen entrance fee.

Shuttle buses depart from Terminal 1 (first floor, stop No. 30) and Terminal 2 (third floor, stop No. 2) for the museum. The trip takes 15 minutes and costs 200 yen. There are only four buses per day. Alternatively, a taxi ride from the airport costs about 1600 yen.

Tokyo Haneda Airport

(see separate entry)

Airports in Malaysia & Singapore

1. Kuala Lumpur International Airport
2. Singapore Changi International Airport

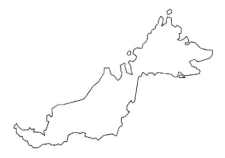

This page has been intentionally left blank.

Kuala Lumpur International, Malaysia

KUL | WMKK
Tel: +603 8776 2000
Web: www.klia.com.my
Passengers: 29,682,093 (2009)

Overview

Kuala Lumpur International, or KLIA as it is known to locals and regulars, is one of Asia's busiest airports. It was opened in 1998, replacing the cramped Subang Airport close to the centre of the city, and enabled Malaysia's capital to handle a lot more passenger and cargo traffic and gave Malaysia Airlines room to breathe.

The airport has a main terminal building with four-pier satellite terminal. The Low Cost Carrier Terminal opened in 2006, and the airport plans to open Terminal 2 in 2012. It has two runways, and a large cargo complex. Most of the Asia and Europe's major airlines operate into KLIA, however airlines from the Americas are lacking.

Spotting Locations

1. Terminal Viewing Gallery

Upstairs in the main terminal building, close to the food court, is the airport's official viewing area. Situated indoors, this large room overlooks the airfield, including all gates at the main building, and some of those on the satellite terminal. The Cargo and Low Cost terminals are not really visible from this area, and the runways are a little distant. But most movements will be visible at some point. Photography can sometimes take a hit because of the glass, but in general is quite good.

2. Runway 32L

Instead of driving to the Low Cost Terminal and Cargo area, continue along the road which passes the end of runway 32L. Just past here is a place to park by the side of the road. This spot is good for landing shots of aircraft using this runway, and gives you views across to some of the aprons not visible from the official viewing gallery. You can continue further along the road to get more views across the airfield, and will eventually reach the main terminal area.

MAP

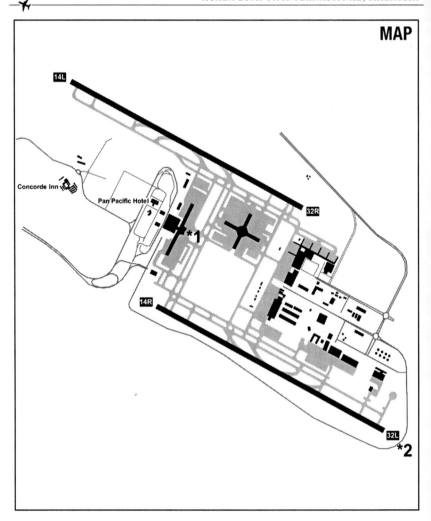

Frequencies

Tower	118.5
Tower	118.8
Ground	121.65
Ground	121.8
Ground	122.15
Ground	122.85
Clearance Delivery	126.0
Approach	119.45
Approach	124.2
Approach	125.1
ATIS	126.45

Runways

14L/32R 13,530ft / 4,124m
14R/32L 13,288ft / 4,056m

Airlines

Air Arabia	Firefly	Oman Air
Air Astana	Gading Sari	Pakistan International
Air China	Garuda Indonesia	Airlines
Air India Express	GMG Airlines	Qatar Airways
Air Mauritius	Gulf Air	Republic Express
Air Niugini	Indonesia AirAsia	Royal Brunei Airlines
Air Zimbabwe	Iran Air	Royal Jordanian
AirAsia	Japan Airlines	Saudi Arabian Airlines
AirAsia X	Jet Airways	SilkAir
Biman Bangladesh	Jetstar Asia Airways	Singapore Airlines
Airlines	KLM	Singapore Airlines Cargo
Cargolux	Korean Air	SriLankan Airlines
Cathay Pacific	Korean Air Cargo	Thai AirAsia
Cebu Pacific	Kuwait Airways	Thai Airways International
China Airlines	Lion Air	Tiger Airways
China Airlines Cargo	Lufthansa	TNT Airways
China Southern Airlines	Lufthansa Cargo	Transmile Air Services
China Eastern Airlines	Mahan Air	Tri-MG Intra Asia Airlines
Coyne Airways	Malaysia Airlines	Turkish Airlines
DHL	MASkargo	United Airways
EgyptAir	Merpati Nusantara	UPS Airlines
Emirates	Airlines	Uzbekistan Airways
Etihad Airways	Myanmar Airways	Vietnam Airlines
EVA Air	International	Xiamen Airlines
EVA Air Cargo	Nepal Airlines	Yemenia
FedEx Express	Nippon Cargo Airlines	

Hotels

Pan Pacific Hotel KLIA

Jalan CTA 4B, 64000 KLIA - Sepang | +603 8787 3333 | www.panpacific.com

Situated next to the control tower and main terminal building (and linked via a covered bridge), the Pan Pacific is a favourite amongst spotters. Higher floor rooms offer some views across the terminal ramps and of runway 14L/32R.

Concorde Inn

Jalan KLIA 1/60 43900 KLIA - Sepang | +603 8783 3118 | sepang.concordehotelsresorts.com

A pleasant resort hotel only five minutes from the main terminal at KLIA, and often more affordable than the Pan Pacific. It doesn't really have any useful views of movements, although aircraft using runway 14R/32L pass almost overhead at height. This isn't a problem, as the viewing gallery is close enough, and night time movements can be checked using SBS if you have one.

Nearby Attractions

Subang Airport

Now named Sultan Abdul Aziz Shah Airport, the original Kuala Lumpur Subang is still an operational airport, albeit a shadow of its former self. The main terminal was demolished when KLIA opened, but its former Terminal 3 is now operating as a domestic and charter terminal for flights. The airport is also home to a busy cargo terminal and maintenance base. Eurocopter Malaysia is also based here. The airport is around a 30 minute drive from KLIA, and most aircraft can be seen by driving around the access and perimeter roads.

Singapore Changi International Airport, Singapore

SIN | WSSS

Tel: +65 6595 6868
Web: www.changiairport.com
Passengers: 37,203,978 (2009)

Overview

Changi Airport is one of the world's biggest aviation hubs, and a major transit point for travellers heading between Europe and Asia. Home to the large Singapore Airlines and its cargo division, the airport is rarely quiet and offers an interesting mix for the enthusiast. Changi is a hub for the A380 aircraft, used here by a variety of airlines.

There are two parallel runways in use for the airport, with a third located a mile to the east and not yet used in day-to-day operations, but will one day be incorporated into the airport as it expands. There are currently three terminals in use, plus a budget terminal, and another planned for the future.

In addition to being one of the busiest airports in the world for passengers, Changi is also a busy cargo hub and base for the Singapore Air Force's fleet of transport aircraft. Maintenance of Singapore Airlines and some other airlines' aircraft is also carried out here.

Spotting Locations

1. Terminal 1 Viewing Mall

Nicely air-conditioned, you can enjoy some good views of movements from this indoor area which only opened in late 2010. It has views of the central apron and more distant views of aircraft on the runways. Singapore Airlines aircraft don't usually park here. Photography is acceptable, but through glass. To reach the area, go one up the escalators from the check-in hall.

2. Terminal 2 Viewing Mall

Smaller than the Terminal 1 Mall, this is another indoor room which looks out over parking stands used by Singapore Airlines and some other airlines, plus runway 02C/20C. You can reach this area by heading up the escalators to the floor above departures, following the signs. Again, photography is possible through glass.

MAP

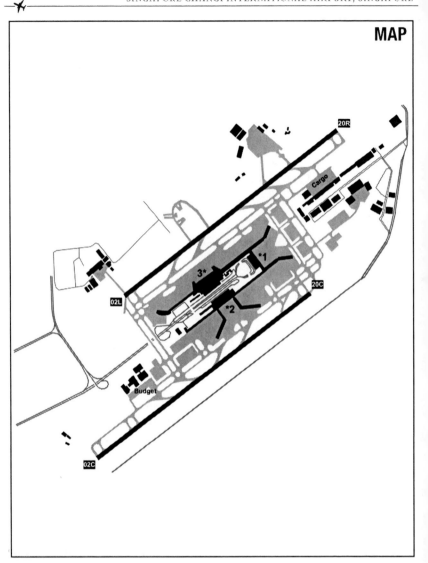

Frequencies

Tower	118.6
Tower	121.85
Ground	121.725
Ground	124.3
Clearance Delivery	121.65
Arrivals	119.3
Approach	120.3
ATIS	128.6

Runways

2L/20R	13,123ft / 4,000m
2C/20C	13,123ft / 4,000m
2R/20L	9,022ft / 2,750m (not on map)

3. Terminal 3 Viewing Mall

This indoor area looks out over runway 02L/20R, which is usually the arrivals runway. Photography is not good here, but you can still log movements with ease. Reach the area from the check-in area via escalators, following the signs.

Airlines

Aerologic
Air China
Air France
Air Hong Kong
Air India (Indian)
Air India Express
Air Macau
Air Mauritius
Air Niugini
Air Seychelles
AirAsia
Airphil Express
All Nippon Airways
Asiana Airlines
Asiana Cargo
Bangkok Airways
Batavia Air
Berjaya Air
Biman Bangladesh
Airlines
British Airways
Cardig Air
Cargolux
Cathay Pacific
Cathay Pacific Cargo
Cebu Pacific
China Airlines
China Airlines Cargo
China Eastern Airlines
China Southern Airlines

Delta Air Lines
Emirates
Etihad Airways
EVA Air
EVA Air Cargo
FedEx Express
Finnair
Firefly
Garuda Indonesia
Hainan Airlines
Hong Kong Airlines
Indonesia AirAsia
Japan Airlines
Jet Airways
Jetstar Airways
Jetstar Asia Airways
Jett8 Airlines Cargo
Kingfisher Airlines
KLM
KLM Cargo
Korean Air
Korean Air Cargo
Lion Air
Lufthansa
Lufthansa Cargo
Malaysia Airlines
Mandala Airlines
Martinair Cargo
MASkargo
Myanmar Airways

International
Nippon Cargo Airlines
Philippine Airlines
Qantas
Qatar Airways
Republic Express Airlines
Royal Brunei Airlines
Saudi Arabian Airlines
Shanghai Airlines Cargo
SilkAir
Singapore Airlines
Singapore Airlines Cargo
South East Asian Airlines
SriLankan Airlines
Sriwijaya Air
Thai AirAsia
Thai Airways International
Tiger Airways
TNT Airways
Transaero Airlines
Transmile Air Services
Tri-MG Intra Asia Airlines
Turkish Airlines
United Airlines
UPS Airlines
Valuair
Vietnam Airlines
Xiamen Airlines

Hotels

Crowne Plaza

75 Airport Boulevard #01-01, Singapore 819664 | +65 6823 5300 | www.crowneplaza.com

The best hotel for spotting at Singapore Changi, but can be expensive. Views from the rooms even numbered are excellent if you get one on floors 7, 8 or 9 facing the airport.

You will have views of some terminal 3 gates and the main runway. Corridors can also be used for views of the central terminal area.

Changi Village Hotel

1 Netheravon Road, Singapore 508502 | +65 6379 7111 | www.stayvillage.com/changi/

If you ask for a room facing the sea, you will be able to read off arriving aircraft landing on runway 20R and see aircraft using 20L, or 02L/R. An SBS is useful for night time movements. Again this is another fairly expensive hotel.

Nearby Attractions

Seletar Airport

Around ten miles from Changi, Seletar is a small airport which was the first airport for Singapore but spent most of its life as an RAF base. Despite trying in the past, there are no scheduled passenger flights currently. The airport is principally used by light aircraft, however you will often find airliners in for cargo flights and maintenance work. You can easily note aircraft parked on the main apron from the access road leading to the terminal.

Paya Lebar Air Base

Paya Lebar was Singapore's main airport until Changi opened in 1981, and handled the famous Concorde flights in a joint venture between British Airways and Singapore Airlines. It had become very restricted as passenger numbers grew to 4 million per year. Following this, the airport became a military base. It is also used today for aircraft maintenance, and one or two airliners can often be found on the ground. Distant views are possible from the road next to the Air Force Museum:

Air Force Museum

400 Airport Road, Singapore 534234
www.mindef.gov.sg/imindef/mindef_websites/atozlistings/air_force/about/museum.html

Charting the history of the Royal Singapore Air Force through a number of displays and aircraft exhibits. Aircraft are displayed on the ground, and also suspended from the ceiling, and all in immaculate condition. Open 8.30am-5pm daily except Monday and public holidays. Free admission.

Airports in New Zealand

1. Auckland International Airport
2. Christchurch International Airport
3. Wellington International Airport

This page has been intentionally left blank.

Auckland International, New Zealand

AKL | NZAA

Tel: +64 9 275 0789
Web: www.aucklandairport.co.nz
Passengers: 13,202,772 (2008)

Overview

Auckland is the busiest airport in New Zealand, and the principal gateway to the country. It is also the main base of national carrier Air New Zealand and its worldwide flight network. The airport officially has two runways, however one is used most of the time as a parallel taxiway and backup.

There are two terminals at Auckland - the International Terminal to the west, and the smaller Domestic Terminal to the east. Further east is an area of freight aprons and maintenance hangars. For the enthusiast, a number of viewing locations are provided, and a good mix of airliners pass through every day.

Spotting Locations

1. International Terminal Observation Area

Situated upstairs in the International Terminal, this enclosed lounge has great views over all movements at the airport and on the runway. Photography is not the best from this location due to the glass. A staircase leads to a room on the top floor with slightly more elevated views.

2. Domestic Terminal Observation Area

This area is outdoors, but has a glass frontage so again is not perfect for photography. However, aircraft using the domestic terminal are much closer here, as is the runway. There are no views to the International Terminal from here.

3. Laurence Stevens Drive

This road runs east from the roundabout outside the Domestic Terminal and leads you past the cargo and maintenance aprons. Delving into the various gaps between buildings will yield many of the aircraft parked out of view of the terminal observation areas.

MAP

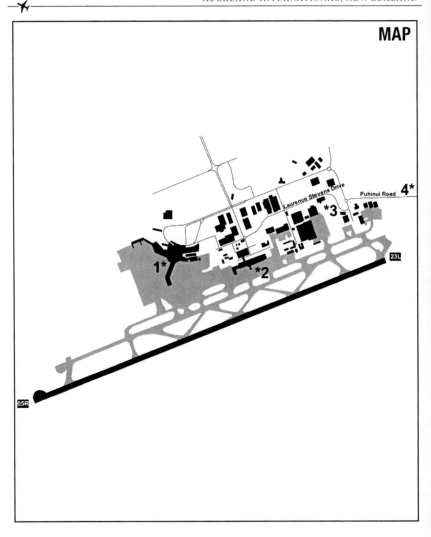

Frequencies

Ground	121.9
Tower	118.7
Tower	120.8
Approach	124.3
Approach	129.5
Approach	129.6
Clearance Delivery	128.2
ATIS	127.8
ATIS	127.0

Runways

5R/23L 11,926ft / 3,635m
5L/23R 10,197ft / 3,108m (reserve)

4. Puhinui Road Viewing Area

A viewing area is available just off the Puhinui Road as it runs east away from the airport. There are car parking spaces on either side of the road. The elevated position makes it a great spot for watching and photographing arrivals on runway 23.

Airlines

Aerolineas Argentinas
Air Chathams
Aircalin
Airwork
Air Freight NZ
Air New Zealand
Air New Zealand Link (Air Nelson)
Air New Zealand Link (Eagle Airways)
Air New Zealand Link (Mount Cook Airline)
Air Pacific
Air Tahiti Nui
Air Vanuatu
Cargolux
Cathay Pacific
China Southern Airlines
Continental Airlines
DHL
Emirates
FedEx Express
Great Barrier Airlines
Jetstar Airways
Jetstar Asia Airways
Korean Air
LAN Airlines
Lufthansa Cargo
Malaysia Airlines
Mountain Air
Pacific Blue
Polynesian Blue
Qantas
Qantas (Jetconnect)
Royal Brunei Airlines
Singapore Airlines
Thai Airways International

Hotels

Grand Chancellor Hotel

Kirkbride/Ascot Roads, Airport Oaks, Auckland | +64 (9) 275 7029 | www.ghihotels.com

Sadly none of the rooms have views of aircraft, but this hotel is quite convenient with a free courtesy bus. The hotel's car park has distant views of aircraft.

Nearby Attractions

Ardmore Airport

This former WWII USAF bomber base is now a general aviation airfield around 15 miles east of Auckland International. It has a single runway and is the busiest airport in New Zealand by number of movements. Mountain Air has their maintenance base here, and there is a warbird restoration company in residence with a number of aircraft.

North Shore Airfield

Situated 16 miles north of Auckland city centre. It is a small general aviation field which is popular for flight training. Movements can be seen from Postman Rd which also runs past the parking aprons.

Christchurch International Airport, New Zealand

CHC | NZCH

Tel: +64 358 5029
Web: www.christchurchairport.co.nz/
Passengers: 6,037,729 (2008)

Overview

Christchurch is the busiest airport on the South Island and handles a lot of domestic traffic, plus international routes from Australia and the Far East. It has two runways and a two passenger terminals. However, the Domestic Terminal is due to be demolished and replaced by the new structure which is being built at the time of writing.

Spotting Locations

1. Perimeter Road

This road runs east from the terminal. Turn right onto Ron Guthrey Rd, and then right onto Avonhead Rd. Following this will lead you to numerous vantage points over the runways and terminal, which will be adequate for some nice photographs. Follow it onto Grays Rd and Pound Rd. It leads to Jessons Rd, which has a vantage point at the end.

2. Orchard Road

Following this road away from the terminals will pass the various cargo, military and maintenance ramps. Occasional vantage points for photography are available, but don't loiter too long.

Airlines

Air Chathams	Air Transport International
Air New Zealand	Emirates
Air New Zealand Link (Air National)	Jetstar Airways
Air New Zealand Link (Air Nelson)	Pacific Blue
Air New Zealand Link (Eagle airways)	Qantas
Air New Zealand Link (Mount Cook Airline)	Singapore Airlines
Air Pacific	

MAP

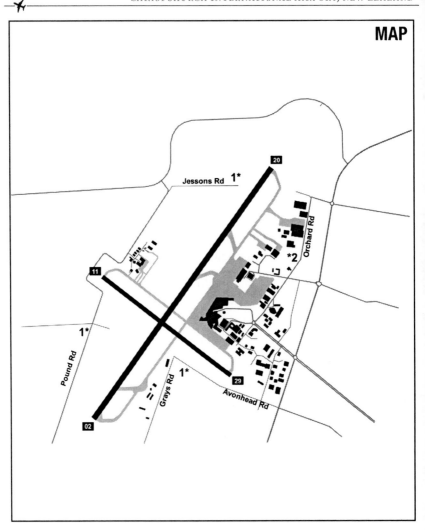

Frequencies

Tower	118.3
Tower	125.0
Ground	121.9
Ground	125.0
Approach	120.9
Approach	124.1
Approach	126.1
ATIS	127.2

Runways

2/20 10,785ft / 3,288m
11/29 5,712ft / 1,741m

Hotels

Sudima Hotel

550 Memorial Ave, Christchurch 8053 | +64 (3) 358 3139 | www.sudimachristchurch.co.nz

No views available from this hotel, but it is situated just outside the terminals so couldn't be closer. Ideal for those exploring the views around the terminal area. Rooms are reasonably priced.

Nearby Attractions

Wigram Air force Museum

45 Harvard Ave, Wigram, Christchurch | +64 3 343 9532 | www.airforcemuseum.co.nz

This museum located in Christchurch preserves historic military aircraft and aviation artefacts from New Zealand's past. There are around 30 aircraft, including an Avro Anson and C-47 Dakota.

This page has been intentionally left blank.

Wellington International Airport, New Zealand

WLG | NZWN

Tel: +64 4 385 5100
Web: www.wellington-airport.co.nz
Passengers: 5,021,000 (2008)

Overview

Wellington is the capital city of New Zealand, but isn't anywhere near as large or busy as Auckland. Nevertheless, its small airport - hemmed in between bays to the north and south - is a busy little place. The passenger terminal is on the eastern side of the runway, whilst the opposite side has a general aviation and FBO ramp.

Traffic at Wellington is comprised mainly of domestic flights and flights to Australia. It is a very busy transfer point between the North Island and South Island.

Spotting Locations

1. Perimeter Road

Lyall Parade passes Lyall Bay and then loops round past the end of runway 34 as it passes under the tunnel towards the terminal and Moa Point. Just before it goes under the tunnel, you can stop by the side of the road and get excellent shots of aircraft landing on 34 or lining up for departure. It is best to leave your car at the car park next to the beach where the road starts to loop around the runway.

2. Subway Entrance

A subway links the Rongotai area with the passenger terminal side of the airport. From the entrance you have an excellent view over the runway and general aviation ramp. To reach the spot from the car park at spot 1, head north at the roundabout and turn right on Coutts St. Follow to the end.

3. Terminal

The passenger terminal has some excellent viewpoints from the windows in the piers. Head for the domestic gates.

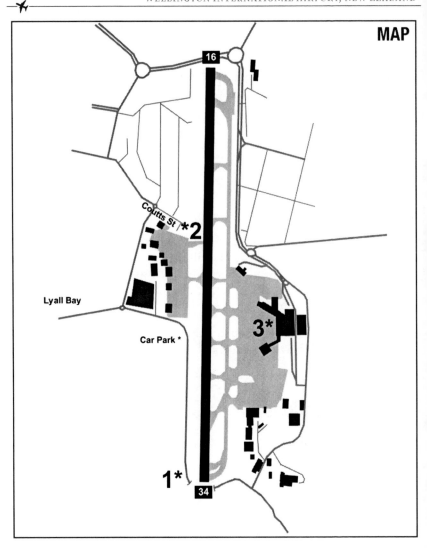

MAP

Frequencies

Tower	118.8
Tower	120.0
Ground	118.8
Ground	121.9
Approach	119.3
Approach	121.1
Approach	122.3
Approach	126.5
ATIS	126.9

Runways
16/34   6,351ft / 1,934m

Airlines

Air Chathams
Air New Zealand
Air New Zealand (Air Nelson)
Air New Zealand (Eagle Airways)
Air New Zealand (Mount Cook Airline)
air2there
Golden Bay Air
Jetstar Airways
Pacific Blue
Qantas (Jetconnect)
Sounds Air

Hotels

Airport Motor Lodge

Hobart Street, Wellington 6022 | +64 4 380 6044 | www.airportmotorlodge.co.nz

An affordable little motel, and the closest lodgings to Wellington Airport. It doesn't have any views of movements, but a short walk down the street brings you to the perimeter fence or the airport terminal. Has free courtesy bus also.

Nearby Attractions

N/A

This page has been intentionally left blank.

Airports in Philippines

1. Manila Ninoy Aquino Airport

This page has been intentionally left blank.

Manila Ninoy Aquino Airport, Philippines

MNL | RPLL

Web: www.miaa.gov.ph

Passengers: 24,108,825 (2009)

Overview

The principal airport in the Philippines, Manila's Ninoy Aquino is one of the busiest in the world and also base for Philippine Airlines. The airport has four terminals, with the newer, modern Terminal 3 along the eastern side of the airport.

Manila has numerous nooks and crannies around the north, east and western sides, which cater to the storage and maintenance of various aircraft from times gone by which will undoubtedly be of interest to the enthusiast. Finding a position to log them is difficult, however.

Spotting Locations

1. Nayong Park

This large park is situated alongside the 13/31 runway. It has a small entrance fee, but is the best place to get close to the action. Photography is good here, also. Be careful as armed guards can often be found in the park. Make sure you explore all areas, as different stored aircraft can be seen from different parts of the park.

2. Multinational Avenue

This road passes the end of runway 6 and you can get good views of aircraft landing, lining up and taking off from here, albeit through the fence. It is a short distance from Terminal 1.

3. Domestic Terminal

The small Manila Domestic Terminal at the north western corner of the airport is one of the few places with any views over the various storage areas across the northern perimeter of the airport. Various windows fronting the apron look out over these aircraft.

MAP

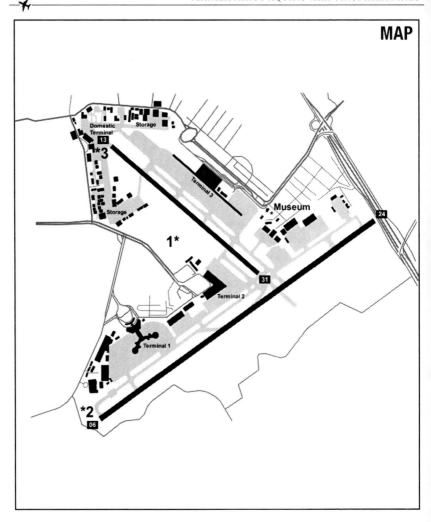

Frequencies

Tower	118.1
Ground	121.9
Ramp 1	121.6
Ramp 1	121.7
Ramp 2	128.8
Domestic Ramp	123.25
Clearance Delivery	125.1
Approach 119.7	
Approach 121.1	
Control 128.3	
ATIS	126.4

Runways

6/24   12,261ft / 3,737m
13/31   7,408ft / 2,258m

Airlines

Air China	Japan Airlines
Air Hong Kong	Jetstar Asia Airways
Air Niugini	KLM
Airphil Express	Korean Air
All Nippon Airways	Korean Air Cargo
Asiana Airlines	Kuwait Airways
Cathay Pacific	Malaysia Airlines
Cebu Pacific	Philippine Airlines
China Airlines	Qantas
China Airlines Cargo	Qatar Airways
China Southern Airlines	Royal Brunei
Continental Micronesia	Saudi Arabian Airlines
Delta Air Lines	Shenzhen Donghai Airlines
Dragonair	South East Asian Airlines
Emirates	Thai Airways International
Etihad Airways	Tiger Airways
EVA Air	Transmile Air Services
FedEx Express	ULS Airlines Cargo
Gulf Air	Yangtze River Express
Hawaiian Airlines	Zest Airways
Hong Kong Express Airways	

Hotels

Courtyard by Marriott
90-10 Grand Central Parkway, East Elmhurst, NY 11369 | (718) 446-4800 | www.marriott.com

Nearby Attractions

Philippine Air Force Museum
Nr Andrews Ave, Pasay City, Manila | +63 2832 3498
www.paf.mil.ph/UNITS/pafmuseum/pafmuseum.html

Located near Terminal 3 on the Villamor Air Base side of the airport. This museum has around 20 aircraft on display, including both fighters and transport types. Open 8am-12pm Mon-Sat. Admission PHP20 per persion.

This page has been intentionally left blank.

Airports in South Korea

1. Seoul Gimpo Airport
2. Seoul Incheon Airport

This page has been intentionally left blank.

Seoul Gimpo Airport, South Korea

GMP | RKSS

Tel: +82 2 2660 2114
Web: gimpo.airport.co.kr
Passengers: 15,369,944 (2009)

Overview

Gimpo was Seoul's main airport from the 1950s until it was superseded by the new Incheon airport in 2001. It is sited much closer to the city, and today is the main domestic airport (although it does handle some international flights, and Incheon also handles some domestic flights). Unlike Incheon, Gimpo has facilities for spotters to view aircraft movements, which include many of the smaller types in the Korean Air and Asiana Airlines fleets. However, due to the sensitive security in the country, aircraft photography and loitering away from the official areas is likely to cause problems.

Gimpo has two parallel runways and both an international and domestic terminal. On the far side of the runways is an air force base.

Spotting Locations

1. Observation Decks

The official observation decks are located in the domestic terminal, on the 6th floor. Both an indoor and outdoor deck is available, with the air conditioned indoor one being a welcome break in the heat of the summer. Both have excellent views over the domestic terminal and runways. You can't see the international terminal, but traffic will taxi past. Signs warn that photography is not allowed.

Airlines

Air Busan	Jin Air
All Nippon Airways	Korea Express Air
Asiana Airlines	Korean Air
China Eastern Airlines	Shanghai Airlines
Eastar Jet	
Japan Airlines	
Jeju Air	

MAP

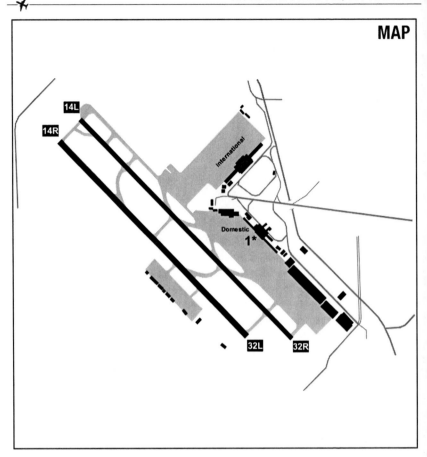

Frequencies

Tower	118.1
Tower	118.05
Ground	121.9
Ground	121.25
Ground	121.95
Clearance Delivery	122.6
Clearance Delivery	125.85
Approach	119.75
Approach	119.9
Approach	120.8
Approach	125.5
Departure	124.8
Departure	125.15
Radar	127.1
ATIS	126.4

Runways

14L/32R   11,811ft / 3,600m
14R/32L   10,499ft / 3,600m

Hotels

There are no hotels at Gimpo airport. It is best to choose one of the options at Incheon if you are looking for a spotting hotel.

Nearby Attractions

Seoul Incheon Airport

(see separate entry)

This page has been intentionally left blank.

Seoul Incheon Airport, South Korea

ICN | RKSI

Tel: +82 32 741 0114
Web: www.airport.kr/eng/
Passengers: 30,000,000 (2009)

Overview

Seoul Incheon was opened in March 2001 after it became apparent the previous Gimpo airport was bursting at the seams and unable to expand. Incheon is a modern airport and has recently opened its third parallel runway and a remote concourse to its terminal. Passenger traffic is busy, with a heavy presence of both Korean Air and Asiana Airlines. Elsewhere, the airport has six cargo terminals on the opposite side of the runways, and proves to be a very busy operation.

Security in South Korea is very tight and aircraft spotters are not officially tolerated. Therefore beware that you are likely to be moved on or told to stop spotting by security personnel. Using binoculars, poles and cameras will only add suspicion, so be very discrete.

Spotting Locations

1. Outside Domestic Terminal

Just outside the domestic terminal there is a smoking area which offers some views over the domestic gates and aircraft approaching runways 33L/R. You can also see aircraft departing in the opposite direction. It is possible to take photographs discretely from here.

2. Panorama Restaurant

Up on the 4th floor of the international part of the terminal is the Panorama Restaurant which has views out over the gates around the terminal, and across to the new concourse. You must buy food and drink if you wish to stay here, and it can be quite expensive.

3. Airside

Once airside in any part of the terminal, there are plenty of places to view aircraft movements. The new concourse is also good for watching. Be aware of the heightened security presence, however.

MAP

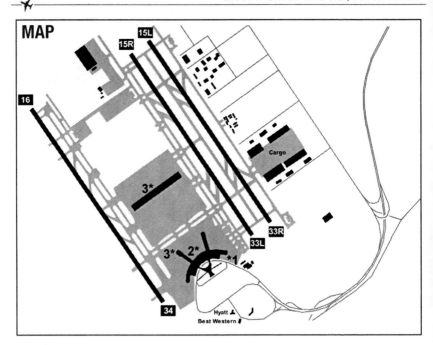

Frequencies

Tower	118.2
Tower	118.275
Tower	118.8
Ground	118.75
Ground	121.7
Ground	121.75
Ramp Control	121.65
Ramp Control	121.625
Ramp Control	121.8
Ramp Control	121.875
Clearance Delivery	118.75
Clearance Delivery	121.6
Approach	119.1
Approach	119.75
Approach	120.8
Approach	121.35
Approach	121.4
Departure	119.05
Departure	124.8
Departure	125.15
ATIS	128.4
ATIS	128.65

Runways

15R/33L	12,303ft / 3,750m
15L/33R	12,303ft / 3,750m
16/34	13,123ft / 4,000m

Airlines

Aeroflot
Aeroflot-Cargo
AeroLogic
Air Astana
Air Canada
Air China
Air China Cargo
Air France
Air Hong Kong
Air India
Air Macau
AirAsia X
AirBridgeCargo Airlines
Aircalin
All Nippon Airways
ANA & JP Express
ANA Cargo
Aryan Cargo Express
Asiana Airlines
Asiana Cargo
Atlant-Soyuz Airlines
Atlas Air
Aviacon Zitotrans
British Airways World Cargo
Business Air
Cargolux
Cathay Pacific
Cathay Pacific Cargo
Cebu Pacific
China Airlines
China Airlines Cargo
China Cargo Airlines
China Eastern Airlines
China Postal Airlines
China Southern Airlines
Delta Air Lines
Eastar Jet
Emirates
Etihad Airways
EVA Air
FedEx Express
Finnair
Finnair Cargo
Garuda Indonesia
Great Wall Airlines

Hawaiian Airlines
Hong Kong Express
Jade Cargo International
Japan Airlines
Jeju Air
Jin Air
Kalitta Air
KLM
KLM Cargo
Korean Air
Korean Air Cargo
Lufthansa
Malaysia Airlines
Mandarin Airlines
MASkargo
MIAT Mongolian Airlines
Midex Airlines
Nippon Cargo Airlines
Philippine Airlines
Polar Air Cargo
Polet Airlines
Qantas Freight
Qatar Airways
SAT Airlines
Shandong Airlines
Shanghai Airlines
Shanghai Airlines Cargo
Sichuan Airlines
Singapore Airlines
Singapore Airlines Cargo
Southern Air
Thai Airways International
Tradewinds Airlines
Turkish Airlines
United Airlines
UPS Airlines
Uzbekistan Airways
Vietnam Airlines
Vladivostok Air
Volga-Dnepr Airlines
Xiamen Airlines
World Airways
Yangtze River Express
Zest Airways

Hotels

Hyatt Regency Incheon Hotel

2850-1 Woonseo-Dong, Jung-Gu, Incheon 400-340 | +82 32 745 1234 | incheon.regency.hyatt.com

Located close to the end of runway 33, rooms facing the airport have views of this. Aircraft are quite far, so need a good pair of binoculars to read off. The hotel is fairly expensive. There is a free shuttle bus to the terminal.

Best Western Airport Hotel Incheon

2850 Unseo-Dong, Jung-Gu, Incheon 00000 | +82 32 743 1000 | www.bestwestern.com

Located in a similar position to the Hyatt, it is a little more reasonable but offers the same distant views of runway 33 and views of the terminals from some rooms. In-room TVs have a channel listing arrivals and departures, including cargo and GA movements.

Nearby Attractions

Seoul Gimpo Airport

(see separate entry)

Airports in Thailand

1. Bangkok Don Mueang Airport
2. Bangkok Suvarnabhumi Airport
3. Phuket International Airport

This page has been intentionally left blank.

Bangkok Don Mueang Airport, Thailand

DMK | VTBD

Tel: +66 2535 1111
Web: www2.airportthai.co.th/en/
Passengers: 2,758,831 (2010)

Overview

Don Mueang today is a shadow of its former self - a one large and proud international gateway to Thailand, and hub to the national airline, which has been superseded by the new Suvarnabhumi International, which opened in 2006.

Nevertheless, Don Mueang reopened in 2007 after some renovation, and is now home to domestic flights by a few low-cost airlines, plus charter and military flights. It is still worth visiting when in the city for some rarer aircraft and the chance to visit the Royal Thai Air Force Museum on site.

The airport has two parallel runways, with a golf course running in-between, and has three terminals - although only Terminal 3 is currently in use. There are occasional plans to reopen the other terminals and develop the airport further as a low-cost hub.

Spotting Locations

1. Terminal 1 Car Park

The top floor of this car park is a good place to see aircraft up close at the terminals. Standing too close to the edge is likely to draw attention, however.

2. Terminal Interior

Inside the terminal you can get good views and some chances for photography (through glass) of aircraft. Head for the ends of the piers and move around to make sure you catch everything.

Airlines

Nok Air
Orient Thai Airlines
Solar Air

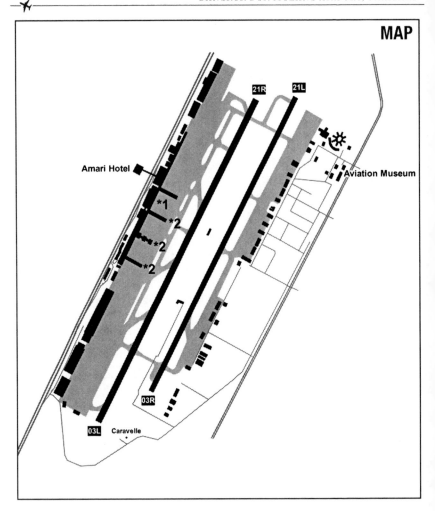

Frequencies

Tower	118.1
Ground	121.9
Ground	122.5
Clearance Delivery	120.4
Clearance Delivery	128.4
Clearance Delivery	133.4
Arrival	125.5
Approach	119.1
Approach	121.7
Approach	127.7
ATIS	126.4

Runways

3L/21R 12,139ft / 3,700m
3R/21L 11,482ft / 3,500m

Hotels

Amari Don Muang Bangkok

333 Chert Wudthakas Road, Bangkok 10210 | +66 2566 1020 | www.amari.com/donmuang/

A smart, elegant international-standard hotel situated over the road from Terminal 1. It is linked by a walkway to the airport. The hotel can be expensive, and doesn't really offer any views of aircraft.

Nearby Attractions

Royal Thai Air Force Museum

Thanon-Phahon Yothin, Bangkok | +66 2534 1853 | rtaf.mi.th/museum/

Located on the opposite side of the runways to the terminal. This museum has over 400 aircraft in one state or another, covering all aspects of the country's air force history. The ones on display are in excellent condition. Open daily 8am-4pm, admission free. Buses stop here, but it's best to get a taxi.

Bangkok Suvarnabhumi Airport

(see separate entry)

This page has been intentionally left blank.

Bangkok Suvarnabhumi Airport

Thailand

BKK I VTBS

Tel: +66 2132 1888

Web: www.suvarnabhumiairport.com

Passengers: 40,500,000 (2009)

Overview

Suvarnabhumi is Bangkok's new International Airport. It was opened in September 2006 to replace the cramped and ageing Don Mueang Airport. The land had actually been purchased in the 1970s in the knowledge that a replacement airport would be needed, but various delays meant it wasn't until 1996 that serious plans were made.

The airport is one of the busiest in Asia (and the world), and has the world's tallest control tower at 132m (432ft). It currently has one large terminal, but is already well into the planning phases for two new runways, remote terminal piers, a low-cost terminal, and a new terminal building to the south which mirrors the existing one.

Suvarnabhumi is certainly a very busy airport which handles a lot of movements and passengers every year. It can be a delight for spotters.

Spotting Locations

1. Observation Area

Inside the terminal is an area set aside for watching aircraft. The views are good and photography is possible with a long lens. Having nearby eateries and coffee shop also makes this a comfortable place to watch aircraft. You will not see the whole apron, but most movements will be visible at some point.

2. Western Perimeter

A small road runs along the length of the western airfield perimeter, following alongside runway 1L/19R and the planned third runway site. It is possible to pull over here and take photos or log what is visible parked at the terminal and, further north, the cargo terminal. A long lens is needed. Accessible off Rom Klao Road.

MAP

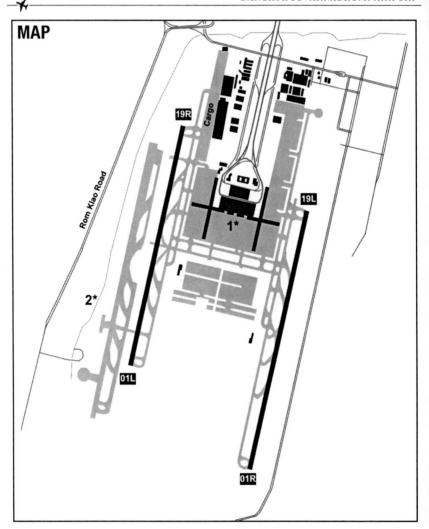

Frequencies

Tower	118.2
Tower	119.0
Ground	121.65
Ground	121.75
Ground	121.95
Arrivals	124.7
Approach	122.35
Approach	124.35
Approach	125.2

Runways

1L/19R	12,139ft / 3,700m
1R/19L	13,123ft / 4,000m

Airlines

Aeroflot
Aerosvit Airlines
Air Astana
Air Austral
Air Berlin
Air China
Air Finland
Air France
Air France Cargo
Air Hong Kong
Air India (Indian)
Air India Express
Air Italy Polska
Air Koryo
Air Macau
Air Madagascar
AirAsia
All Nippon Airways
ANA Cargo
Asiana Airlines
Asiana Cargo
Austrian Airlines
Bangkok Airways
Biman Bangladesh
Airlines
Bismillah Airlines
Blue Panorama Airlines
British Airways
Business Air
Cardig Air
Cargolux
Cathay Pacific
Cathay Pacific Cargo
Cebu Pacific
China Airlines
China Airlines Cargo
China Eastern Airlines
China Southern Airlines
Delta Air Lines
DHL
Druk Air
EgyptAir
El Al

Emirates
Emirates SkyCargo
Ethiopian Airlines
Etihad Airways
EVA Air
EVA Air Cargo
FedEx Express
Finnair
FlyLAL Charters
Garuda Indonesia
GMG Airlines
Gulf Air
Hainan Airlines
Happy Air
Hong Kong Airlines
Indonesia AirAsia
Iran Air
Japan Airlines
Jeju Air
Jet Airways
Jetstar Airways
Jetstar Asia Airways
Jett8 Airlines Cargo
Jin Air
K-Mile Air
Kenya Airways
Kingfisher Airlines
KLM
KLM Cargo
Korean Air
Korean Air Cargo
Kuwait Airways
Kuzu Airlines Cargo
Lao Airlines
Lufthansa
Lufthansa Cargo
Mahan Air
Malaysia Airlines
Martinair Cargo
MASkargo
Myanmar Airways
International
Nepal Airlines

Nippon Cargo Airlines
Nordwind Airlines
Oman Air
Orient Thai Airlines
Pakistan International
Airlines
Philippine Airlines
Qantas
Qatar Airways
Royal Brunei Airlines
Royal Jordanian
S7 Airlines
Saudi Arabian
Airlines Cargo
Scandinavian Airlines
Shanghai Airlines
Shanghai Airlines Cargo
Singapore Airlines
Singapore Airlines Cargo
Southern Air
SriLankan Airlines
Swiss International
Air Lines
Thai AirAsia
Thai Airways International
Thomas Cook Airlines
Scandinavia
Tiger Airways
Transaero
Travel Service
Tri-MG Intra Asia Airlines
TUIfly Nordic
Turkish Airlines
Turkmenistan Airlines
UNI Air
United Airlines
UPS Airlines
Ural Airlines
Uzbekistan Airways
Vietnam Airlines
Vladivostok Air
Yanda Airlines
Yangtze River Express

Hotels

Queens Garden Resort

Suvarnabhumi, Lat Krabang, Bangkok 10520 | www.queensgardenresort.net

The best-known hotel for spotting at the new Bangkok airport. Management understand the needs of spotters and will grand access to the rooftop area, and balcony facing final approach to runway 19R. The hotel is only 2 miles from the terminal and very affordable. Ask staff and they can provide you with a list of the day's arrivals.

Nearby Attractions

Bangkok Don Mueang Airport

(see separate entry)

Phuket International Airport, Thailand

HKT | VTSP

Tel: +66 2535 1111
Web: www.airportthai.co.th/phuket/en/
Passengers: 2,900,000 (2009)

Overview

Despite being quite a small airport, Phuket is one of Thailand's main gateways due to the popularity of the island as a tourist resort. As well as a busy air link to Bangkok, Phuket handles flights from across Asia, Australasia and Europe - especially during the summer months. Wide body types are common, as are domestic regional aircraft. The airport has two terminals - one for international and the other domestic flights.

Spotting Locations

1. Nai Yang Beach

The idyllic beach is part of a national park, so is quite unspoilt. When aircraft are arriving from the west, you can get some spectacular shots from this beach. There are also views of aircraft parked at the terminal and lining up on the runway.

2. Terminal

Inside the terminal, once through departures you have views from all gates but will need to move from one end to the other to see all areas of the apron.

Airlines

Aeroflot	Condor
Air Berlin	Dragonair
AirAsia	Edelweiss Air
Asiana Airlines	Finnair
Bangkok Airways	Firefly
Blue Panorama Airlines	Hainan Airlines
China Airlines	Happy Air
China Eastern Airlines	Jetstar Airways
China Southern Airlines	Jetstar Asia Airways

MAP

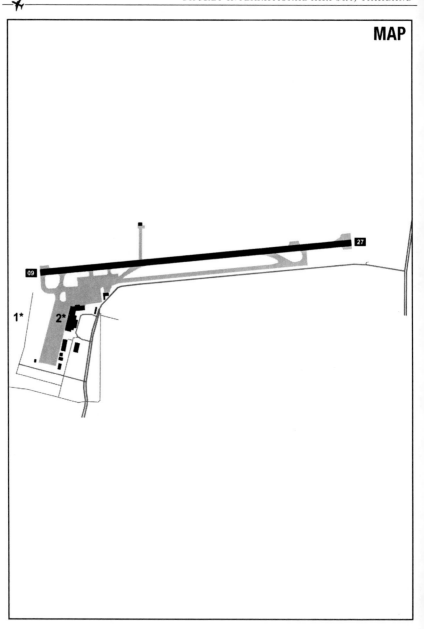

Frequencies

Tower	118.1
Ground	121.9
Approach	124.7
ATIS	128.0

Runways

9/27   9,843ft / 3,000m

Korean Air
Malaysia Airlines
Nok Air
Orient Thai Airlines
Pacific Blue
Qatar Airways
Shanghai Airlines
SilkAir
Strategic Airlines
Thai AirAsia

Thai Airways International
Thomas Cook Airlines Scandinavia
Tiger Airways
Transaero Airlines
TransAsia Airways
TUIfly Nordic
UNI Air
V Australia
XL Airways France

Hotels

Phuket Airport Hotel

90-10 Grand Central Parkway, East Elmhurst, NY 11369 | +66 76 328 451 | www.phuketair-porthotel.com

This is a small but pleasant hotel only 600 metres from the airport. It is not under the flightpath and you can't see movements from the rooms. But it is a short walk to the beach or the airport terminal. Rooms have all the amenities you could want, including free Wi-Fi, and prices are reasonable.

Nearby Attractions

N/A

This page has been intentionally left blank.

Lightning Source UK Ltd.
Milton Keynes UK

176156UK00001B/2/P